Arise • Awake • Achieve •

The Ultimate Guide to Achieve Your Goal

By Sumeet Sadgir

Inspired by the teachings of Swami Vivekananda.

“Arise, awake, and stop not till the goal is reached.”

–Swami Vivekananda

Source: Wikipedia

Dedication

To my *family*, *relatives*, and *friends* who have always believed in me. Special thanks to my ***sister***, whose continuous encouragement and faith in my abilities have helped me a lot.

Acknowledgements

Writing this book has been an amazing journey, and I am deeply grateful to those who have supported and guided me throughout this process. My heartfelt thanks go to everyone who played a role in bringing this project to life.

Firstly, I extend my sincere gratitude to my parents. Their guidance and encouragement have been invaluable, providing me with the clarity and direction needed to navigate through the complexities of writing. Their belief in my vision has been a source of inspiration and motivation. Thank you for your endless patience and support. Their understanding during the long hours of writing was crucial in keeping me grounded. Their belief in me was a constant reminder of why I embarked on this journey, and for that, I am extremely grateful.

A special thank you goes to my sister, whose encouragement and positivity kept me motivated. Her thoughtful conversations and support helped me through moments of self-doubt and uncertainty. The strength of our relationship and her belief in my work were building blocks in completing this book.

I would also like to acknowledge my friends and relatives for their support and resources. Access to their facilities and materials was important for the research and writing process. Your commitment to supporting creative and scholarly work made a significant difference in the realisation of this book.

My thanks also extend to the numerous authors, researchers, and thinkers like Swami Vivekananda, whose work has influenced this book. Their contributions to the field have provided the foundation upon which this work is built. The depth of knowledge and insight from their writings has been instrumental in shaping my understanding and presentation of the subject matter.

Finally, I want to express my appreciation to everyone who has been a part of this journey, even if not mentioned individually. Your support, whether through direct contributions or moral encouragement, has been deeply appreciated. This book is as much a result of your faith in me as it is of my own efforts. In closing, I am deeply grateful to all who have played a part in this amazing journey. Your support has not only made this book possible but has also made this journey incredibly rewarding. Thank you for being a part of this experience and for contributing to the realisation of this dream.

Foreword

I'm so excited for you to get into this book! From the moment I started reading it, I was struck by how seamlessly it brings together the timeless wisdom of Swami Vivekananda with practical advice that's relevant to everyday life. This book isn't just a guide; it feels like having a wise and caring friend by your side, offering support and encouragement every step of the way.

The structure of the book is simple yet incredibly powerful, divided into three key parts: Arise, Awake, and Achieve. Each section is thoughtfully designed to guide you through a specific phase of your journey. You'll begin by preparing yourself physically and mentally in the Arise section, setting the foundation for all that's to come. In the Awake section, you'll move on to awakening your inner potential, tapping into strengths and abilities that you may not even know you have. Finally, in the Achieve section, you'll learn how to reach your goals while staying true to your values and maintaining balance in your life. The steps outlined in each part are clear and actionable, making it easy to follow along and apply the teachings to your own life.

What truly stands out to me about this book is the way it blends practical steps with deeper spiritual insights. It's not just about reaching your goals; it's about growing as a person along the way. The wisdom shared in these pages goes beyond the surface, encouraging you to reflect on your values, cultivate self-awareness, and stay grounded in the midst of life's challenges. This holistic approach ensures that you're not just achieving success in a conventional sense but also experiencing growth and fulfilment on a deeper level.

The advice offered in this book is genuine and straightforward, making it accessible to readers of all backgrounds and experiences. Whether you're just beginning your journey of self-improvement or are already well along the path, you'll find valuable insights and practical strategies that resonate with you. The steps are presented in a way that's easy to understand, yet they're packed with wisdom that can have a profound impact on your life.

As you explore these pages, I encourage you to take your time and immerse yourself in the journey. Embrace the process of growth and transformation, knowing that every step you take is bringing you closer to becoming the best version of yourself. The journey may not always be easy, but with this book as your guide, you'll find the strength and inspiration you need to keep moving forward.

I'm cheering you on every step of the way and can't wait to see the incredible things you'll achieve. Remember, this book isn't just about reaching the finish line; it's about enjoying the journey and learning from every experience along the way. So, take a deep breath, dive in, and let this book be your guide as you enter this exciting adventure of personal growth and achievement. Good luck, and happy reading!

Sincerely,
Snehal S. Sadgir

Preface

To achieve any goal, it takes discipline, perseverance, and a deep commitment. With my experiences in life, I have found that physical preparation, conscious awareness, spiritual approach, and dedication are the building blocks of success. This book is your guide, making you fully prepared physically, mentally, and spiritually to achieve any goal you have chosen. The purpose of this book is to give you an approach, practical strategies, and insights to achieve what may seem impossible.

My dedication to writing this book is deeply influenced by Swami Vivekananda. His intellectual thoughts, spiritual journey, and lifelong contributions have always inspired me. His teachings on the power of the human mind and the importance of self-discipline have guided and encouraged me to share these insights with you. His life was a testament to the potential of the human spirit and mind, and it is this potential that I wish to help you unlock through the pages of this book.

The concepts and practices outlined here are meant to be applied, not just understood. It is through a consistent application that you will see real transformation in your life. You may face challenges along the way, but remember that these challenges are growth opportunities. Every obstacle you encounter is a chance to strengthen your resolve and deepen your commitment to your goals.

One of the key themes you will encounter in this book is the importance of aligning your physical, mental, and spiritual energies.

Success is not just about working hard; it's about working smart, and that requires balance. Physical preparation is important because it gives you the strength and endurance to pursue your goals. Mental preparation is crucial because it helps you stay focused and overcome distractions. Spiritual preparation connects you to a deeper purpose and keeps you grounded when the journey gets tough. As you progress through this book, you will also find that self-reflection is a vital part of the journey. Taking the time to reflect on your actions, thoughts, and emotions allows you to continuously improve and stay on the right path. It helps you identify areas where you may be falling short and allows you to make the necessary adjustments.

I am also grateful to my family, friends, and relatives who believed in me. Their unwavering support and encouragement have been a source of strength throughout this journey. Writing this book has been a deeply fulfilling experience, and it would not have been possible without their love and understanding. I would also like to express my deepest appreciation to my sister, whose constant support has been invaluable. Her belief in me and this project has been a driving force behind the completion of this book.

To the readers of this book, I want to say that this is not just a book; it's a blueprint for your success. It's a guide that will help you navigate the complexities of life and stay true to your goals. The wisdom of ancient teachings combined with modern techniques will give you a realistic approach to achieving your dreams. Whether you are just starting on your journey or are already on the path, this book has something to offer you.

As you read through the chapters, I encourage you to take notes, highlight important points, and most importantly, put the principles into practice. Knowledge is only powerful when it is applied. The exercises and strategies provided are designed to help you build habits that will lead to long-term success. Change doesn't happen overnight, but with persistence and dedication, you will begin to see the fruits of your efforts. I also want to emphasise the importance of community on this journey. Surround yourself with people who support your goals and encourage you to be your best self. The road to success can be lonely at times, but having a strong support system can make all the difference. Share your experiences, learn from others, and don't be afraid to ask for help when you need it.

This book is meant to be a companion on your journey. It is a tool that you can return to whenever you need guidance, inspiration, or motivation. The path to success is not a straight line, and there will be ups and downs along the way. But with the right mindset, tools, and strategies, you can overcome any obstacle and achieve your goals.

Thank you for choosing this book. May it inspire, guide, and make you fully prepared to achieve all your goals. As you begin your incredible journey of reading this book, I encourage you to approach it with an open mind and implement its principles. Many actionable insights, practical advice, strategies, and practices are mentioned throughout the book, which you should implement in your routine to unlock your true potential. Remember, success is not just about reaching the destination; it's about enjoying the journey and growing along the way. Each step you take brings you closer to becoming the best version of yourself. Stay committed, stay focused, and never give up on your dreams. The journey may be challenging, but the rewards are well worth it.

Contents

Introduction

Every great journey begins with a single step, and this book is designed to help you take that step with confidence and clarity. Inspired by the timeless teachings of Swami Vivekananda, this book serves as a guide to help you achieve your goals, whether they're big or small, personal or professional. By integrating practical advice with spiritual wisdom, it aims to provide you with the tools necessary to overcome obstacles, build resilience, and turn your dreams into reality.

Why This Book?

The purpose of this book is simple: to empower you to achieve your dreams by blending actionable steps with profound insights. Swami Vivekananda emphasised the importance of discipline, mental strength, and spiritual awareness, qualities that are essential for anyone striving for success. This book isn't just about ticking off tasks on a list; it's about growing as a person, inside and out. It's about building a life that is both fulfilling and aligned with your deeper values.

This book is divided into three main parts, each designed to guide you through a different phase of your journey.

- **Part 1: Arise** is where it all begins. This section focuses on building a strong foundation, both physically and mentally. You'll learn the importance of discipline, the power of routine, and how taking care of your body sets the stage for everything else in life. Just as a house needs a solid foundation to stand tall, your goals need a disciplined routine to thrive. This part will help you prepare the soil before planting the seeds of your future success.

- **Part 2: Awake** focuses on mental and spiritual growth. Here, you'll explore how to sharpen your mind, focus your thoughts, and connect with something bigger than yourself. This section is all about waking up to your true potential, finding clarity, and learning to harness the power of your mind. When your mind is clear and focused, you can overcome any obstacle and stay on track, no matter how challenging the journey may become.
- **Part 3: Achieve** brings everything together. In this section, you'll learn how to set clear goals, stay motivated, and achieve success without losing sight of your values. It's about turning your dreams into reality, one step at a time, with purpose and integrity. Achieving your goals isn't just about reaching the finish line; it's about how you get there, and staying true to yourself along the way.

Throughout this book, you'll find practical advice, inspiring stories, and real-world examples to guide you. It's not just a guide to reaching your goals; it's a companion on your journey to becoming the best version of yourself.

So, whether you're starting from scratch or refining your path, this book is here to support you. With the teachings of Swami Vivekananda as your guide, you're about to embark on a journey of self-discovery, growth, and achievement.

Part I – ARISE

Chapter 1 – Self-Discipline

Source: Pinterest

"The greatest sin is to think yourself weak."
–Swami Vivekananda

Believe in your strength for self-discipline. When you have confidence in yourself, you're more likely to stay committed to your routine and resist temptations that could hinder your progress. Self-discipline isn't just about following rules; it's about having the inner conviction to push through challenges and stay focused on your goals. Doubting your abilities creates mental barriers that make it harder to maintain self-discipline and achieve success. Embracing your power helps you overcome these barriers, making it easier to stay disciplined and achieve your goals effectively.

Self-discipline is an important step toward achieving success. In this chapter, we will cover it, starting with the next point itself.

Establishing a Routine:

Establishing a routine is an essential part of self-discipline. It can be considered the structure upon which success is built. A well-planned routine will help you manage time effectively, reduce procrastination, and cultivate habits that will lead to personal growth. It's not just about making or following a schedule but about being committed to a lifestyle that promotes consistency, productivity, and well-being.

It's hard to achieve your entire routine at once and can often lead to burnout. Start small by focusing on one or two key habits you want to include in your routine. For example, if you want to improve your physical health, begin with a daily 10-minute morning workout. Gradually, you can add more elements as your body becomes familiar with these habits. The power of a successful routine lies in consistency, not perfection. There will be days when your routine may get disrupted. Don't let that discourage you. Instead of getting discouraged, adapt and return to your planned routine as soon as possible.

To make your routine more effective, prioritise tasks based on their importance. The Eisenhower Matrix is a helpful method for this. It involves categorising tasks into four quadrants: urgent and important, important but not urgent, urgent but not important, and neither urgent nor important. This technique will help you and ensure that you focus on what truly matters. Time blocking is a technique where you assign specific periods of your day to different activities, such as work, exercise, meals, relaxation, and sleep. By assigning time slots to each of your daily tasks, you prevent activities from overlapping and ensure that each activity gets the time and attention it deserves. This technique can be more effective for those who struggle with time management.

Start and end your day with a consistent routine that includes specific activities suited to the respective time of the day. A morning ritual might involve meditation, exercise, or journaling, setting a positive tone for the day. An evening ritual could include activities like reading, reflecting on the day, or planning for the next day. These rituals provide a good structure and help you in a smooth transition between different phases of the day. Having someone like a friend, family member, or coach to share your routine with can be a powerful motivator. Sharing your goals and routine with someone provides the support and encouragement you need to stay on track. It's important to keep your routine flexible. Your routine should adapt to changes in your circumstances. Regularly analyse your routine, check what's working and what isn't, and make necessary adjustments.

Include exercise in your daily routine. It doesn't necessarily mean that you should go to the gym every day. It can be as simple as going for a walk, practising yoga, or engaging in any physical activity that you enjoy. The goal here is to make movement a part of your daily routine. A routine should also include a focus on nutrition. Study or research and plan your meals accordingly to ensure that you're getting a balanced diet rich in fruits, vegetables, lean proteins, and whole grains.

A good sleep during the night is an essential factor for physical and mental well-being. Make a bedtime routine that includes activities promoting relaxation and signals to your body that it's time to sleep. This can include turning off screens an hour before bed, dimming the lights, and engaging in calming activities like reading or meditation.

Staying hydrated (drinking 3-4 litres of water every day) is often overlooked but is another important factor for maintaining physical health. Include regular water intake in your routine. Start your day with a glass of water, carry a water bottle with you, and set reminders throughout the day for drinking water.

Following a routine not only organises your day but also creates a foundation for achieving your goals. A well-planned routine reduces decision fatigue, allowing you to focus your mental energy on more important tasks. It also helps in building discipline, as you commit to following the routine even when life demotivates you. Over time, this discipline will strengthen your willpower and make it easier for you to pursue long-term goals. Additionally, a routine also adds stability and predictability to your life, reducing stress and anxiety. When you know what to expect from your day, you can be well-prepared to handle unexpected challenges. This boosts your confidence and overall well-being.

Establishing a routine is a powerful tool for self-discipline. It prepares the foundation for your personal and professional growth, enabling you to achieve your goals. By starting small, prioritising tasks, and maintaining consistency, you can create a routine that supports your physical health, mental clarity, and spiritual well-being.

The Importance of Early Rising:

Early rising is often mentioned as one of the most effective habits for personal development. It sets the perfect tone for a productive day, offering a calm start, clarity, and control over one's life. The benefits of waking up early are beyond just gaining a few extra hours; it improves your mental, physical, and emotional well-being, making it a powerful tool for self-improvement. This practice, when included in your routine, will help you align your day with your goals and values.

People who rise early often say that the quiet morning hours are the most productive part of their day. With the fewest distractions and interruptions, you can focus on your most important tasks without the noise of the day interfering with your work. By the time others are starting their day, you've already made significant progress, giving yourself a head start. Waking up early gives you time to prepare mentally for your day ahead. Instead of rushing through your morning, you have the opportunity to engage in practices that promote mental clarity. These practices may include meditation, journaling, or simply enjoying a quiet cup of coffee. These activities also help you clear your mind, reduce stress, and set a positive tone for the rest of the day. When your mind is calm and focused, you're prepared to handle challenges and make better decisions.

Early rising also has a positive impact on your physical health. It allows you to include morning exercise in your routine, which is a great way to boost your energy levels, improve your mood, and promote better sleep at night. Morning workouts are particularly effective in triggering your metabolism, helping you burn calories more efficiently. Rising early also gives you time to eat a healthy breakfast, which is essential for maintaining high energy levels and cognitive function. The habit of early rising naturally encourages better sleep hygiene. When you wake up early consistently, your body begins to adjust its internal clock, making it easier to fall asleep at the correct time. This regular sleep pattern helps you regulate your circadian rhythm, which leads to deeper and more restful sleep. Over time, this improved sleep quality enhances your overall health, mood, and cognitive function, making it easier to maintain the early rising habit.

Early mornings provide a quiet space for introspection and reflection. These reflective practices help you stay aligned with your long-term objectives. It's also an excellent time to practice mindfulness, which can improve your mental clarity, focus, and overall sense of well-being. Regular self-reflection in the morning can lead to greater self-awareness and a deeper understanding of your values and priorities. The habit of early rising can help you maintain a consistent routine. A consistent wake-up time anchors your day, making it easier for you to build other positive habits. Over time, this routine becomes second nature, freeing up mental energy for more important tasks. It also reinforces self-discipline, as it requires you to prioritise your long-term well-being over short-term comfort.

Waking up early allows you to connect with the natural world in ways that are often missed by those who rise later. Whether it's watching the sunrise, listening to the birds, or feeling the cool morning air, these experiences can be incredibly grounding and rejuvenating. This connection with nature can reduce stress, enhance your mood, and provide a sense of peace and perspective.

If you're not used to waking up early, start by gradually waking up 15-30 minutes earlier until you reach your desired time. This gradual change prevents your body from feeling shocked by the new routine and makes it easier to accomplish. Make yourself ready for success by preparing for the next day the night before. This could include laying out your clothes, preparing your breakfast, or organising your workspace. Evening preparation reduces decision-making in the morning, allowing you to start your day smoothly and with purpose.

Develop a morning ritual with activities like a quiet cup of coffee, reading a few pages of a book, or engaging in a creative activity.

Having something enjoyable to start your day can motivate you to get out of bed and begin your day on a positive note. To ensure you get enough restful sleep, limit your screen time before bed. The blue light emitted by screens can interfere with your sleep cycle, making it harder to fall asleep and wake up early. Instead, choose calming activities like reading books or listening to soothing music.

Consistent early rising requires a consistent bedtime. You need 7-9 hours of sleep every night. Set a bedtime that allows you to get proper and complete rest. Prioritise your sleep by creating a relaxing evening routine. Stick to your bedtime, even on weekends. Early rising is more than just a habit. It's a lifestyle choice that can make a great impact on every aspect of your life. From increased productivity and better time management to improved mental clarity and emotional well-being, the benefits of waking up early are vast. By making early rising a part of your routine, you make yourself ready for success, creating a strong foundation for achieving your goals and living a balanced, fulfilling life.

Regular Exercise:

Regular exercise is the consistent practice of exercise, which leads to a cascade of positive effects that touch every aspect of life, from physical strength to mental clarity and emotional balance. Unlike sporadic workouts, regular exercise acts on self-discipline, promotes well-being, and fosters a long-term commitment to health. This habit doesn't only build muscle or burn calories but also builds resilience, focus, and a sense of purpose.

One of the primary benefits of regular exercise is that it enhances cardiovascular health. Engaging in activities like running, cycling, or swimming strengthens the heart, improves blood circulation, and helps maintain healthy blood pressure levels. Including this habit in your routine reduces the risk of heart disease, stroke, and other cardiovascular issues. Regular aerobic exercise also improves cholesterol levels, increasing the good HDL cholesterol while reducing the bad LDL cholesterol. Regular exercise, particularly strength training, builds stronger muscles and increases endurance. Weightlifting, bodyweight exercises, and resistance training contribute to muscle growth, improved bone density, and enhanced joint stability. Stronger muscles also support everyday activities, making daily tasks easier and reducing the risk of injury.

Including flexibility exercises in your routine, such as yoga or stretching, enhances your range of motion, reduces stiffness, and improves posture. Flexibility exercises also help prevent injuries by keeping muscles and joints limber. Regular stretching promotes overall physical ease and fluidity in movement. Regular physical activity strengthens the immune system, making the body more efficient at fighting infections and illnesses. Exercise increases the circulation of immune cells, enhancing the body's ability to detect and defeat pathogens. While intense workouts may temporarily suppress immunity, moderate and consistent exercise reduces the frequency of colds and other common infections. Maintaining a regular exercise routine effectively manages weight. Exercise helps burn calories, reduces body fat and supports lean muscle mass, which is crucial for maintaining a healthy metabolic rate. Not just burning calories, regular physical activity also helps regulate appetite and supports healthier eating habits. Combined with a balanced diet, exercise gives great results for weight loss.

One of the most immediate benefits of exercise is its ability to reduce stress. Exercise releases endorphins (the body's natural mood elevators), which help reduce stress and promote a sense of well-being. Whether it's an intense workout or a calming yoga session, exercise reduces tension and anxiety and resets your mental state. Regular exercise also regulates cortisol (the body's stress hormone), reducing feelings of stress over time. Regular exercise has been linked to better cognitive function, including improved memory, focus, and problem-solving abilities. Exercise increases blood flow to the brain, enhancing the delivery of oxygen and nutrients that support brain health. It also stimulates the growth of new neurons and strengthens connections between existing ones, leading to better mental sharpness and cognitive resilience. Over time, regular exercise can help protect against age-related cognitive decline and reduce the risk of neurodegenerative diseases like Alzheimer's.

Exercise is a powerful mood booster, which helps combat depression, anxiety, and other emotional challenges. The release of endorphins during exercise creates natural feelings of happiness and relaxation. Regular exercise improves self-esteem and body image, leading to a more positive relationship with yourself. It also provides a healthy outlet for expressing and managing emotions, which is essential for overall emotional well-being. Regular exercise has a profound impact on sleep quality. Engaging in physical activity during the day helps regulate your sleep-wake cycle, making it easier to fall asleep. Exercise can also reduce symptoms of diseases like insomnia. When your body is tired from physical exertion, you're more likely to experience good sleep. It may seem counterintuitive, but regular exercise actually boosts energy levels. By improving cardiovascular health, exercise enhances the efficiency of your heart and lungs, making daily activities less tiring.

It also increases the production of mitochondria, the energy-producing units in your cells, which leads to greater stamina and vitality. To sustain the habit of regular exercise, include variety and enjoyment in your routine. Engage in different types of exercise to keep things interesting and challenge different muscle groups. Whether it's a combination of strength training, cardio, yoga, or sports, variety prevents boredom and keeps you motivated. Choose activities that you genuinely enjoy, as this increases the likelihood of sticking to your routine long-term. Start with small, realistic goals that can be gradually expanded as your fitness improves. Having goals helps you stay focused and committed to your exercise routine.

While regular exercise is important, it's equally important to listen to your body and avoid overtraining. Pay attention to signs of fatigue, soreness, or injury, and adjust your routine accordingly. Include rest days in your schedule to allow your body to recover and repair.

Balancing exercise with proper rest ensures long-term sustainability and prevents burnout or injury. Maintaining regular exercise can be challenging, especially when motivation gets low. Having a workout partner, joining a fitness group, or enlisting the support of a coach or trainer can provide you with the required encouragement.

Acknowledge and celebrate your progress. Whether it's completing a tough workout, improving your strength, or sticking to your routine for a set period, celebrating these milestones reinforces your commitment to regular exercise. Positive reinforcement helps build confidence and motivates you to continue on your fitness journey. By committing to a consistent routine, you can reap the benefits of improved cardiovascular health, stronger muscles, better cognitive function, and emotional resilience.

Maintaining a Balanced Diet:

A balanced diet provides your body with the essential nutrients it needs to function optimally, supports physical health, enhances cognitive performance, and helps prevent chronic diseases. Achieving a balanced diet involves understanding the nutritional requirements of your body, making better food choices, and practising mindful eating habits. This guide will explore various aspects of maintaining a balanced diet without overlapping with other topics related to health and wellness.

Macronutrients are the building blocks of a balanced diet. A balanced diet requires the proper intake of macronutrients (carbohydrates, proteins, and fats). Carbohydrates are the body's primary energy source, proteins are essential for growth and repair, and fats are necessary for hormone production and cell structure. It's important to include a healthy balance of these macronutrients in your daily meals. Complex carbohydrates like whole grains, lean proteins such as legumes, and healthy fats like those found in avocados and nuts should all be part of your diet. In addition to macronutrients, your body needs a range of vitamins and minerals, collectively known as micronutrients, to support various physiological functions. Vitamins like A, C, D, and E, and minerals such as calcium, potassium, and iron, play vital roles in maintaining your immune system and overall energy levels. A balanced diet includes a variety of foods to ensure you receive adequate amounts of these essential nutrients.

Proper hydration is an important component of a balanced diet. Water plays a key role in digestion, nutrient absorption, temperature regulation, and the elimination of toxins from the body. While water is the best source of hydration, fluids from other sources like herbal teas, milk, and water-rich fruits and vegetables also contribute to your daily water intake. Drinking enough water throughout the day helps maintain energy levels, supports cognitive function, and promotes healthy skin.

Prioritising whole foods over processed options is a fundamental principle of a balanced diet. Whole foods like fruits, vegetables, whole grains, and nuts are rich in essential nutrients and free from harmful additives and preservatives. They provide your body with the necessary fuel to function efficiently and help you avoid the negative health effects associated with processed foods, such as obesity, heart disease, and diabetes. A simple yet effective strategy for maintaining a balanced diet is to incorporate a variety of colours on your plate. Different coloured fruits and vegetables are rich in diverse nutrients and phytochemicals that benefit your health in unique ways. For example, red tomatoes are high in lycopene, which supports heart health, while orange carrots are packed with beta-carotene, essential for vision. A colourful plate ensures a diverse nutrient intake and makes meals more visually appealing.

Eating a balanced diet also involves paying attention to portion sizes and practising moderation. Even healthy foods can contribute to weight gain and other health issues if consumed in excessive quantities. Use portion control strategies, such as using smaller plates or measuring servings, to help regulate your intake. Moderation is key to enjoying a variety of foods without overindulging, ensuring that you meet your nutritional needs without exceeding caloric requirements. Understanding food labels is an important aspect of making informed food choices. Labels provide information on the nutrient content, serving sizes, and ingredients of packaged foods. By reading and comparing labels, you can make healthier choices, such as selecting products with fewer added sugars, sodium, and unhealthy fats. Paying attention to food labels also helps you avoid hidden ingredients and allergens that may compromise your diet. A balanced diet starts with mindful grocery shopping.

Plan your meals in advance and create a shopping list that focuses on whole, nutrient-dense foods. Avoid shopping on an empty stomach, as this can lead to impulsive purchases of unhealthy snacks and processed foods. When shopping, stick to the outer aisles of the store where fresh produce and dairy are typically located, and limit your time in the centre aisles where processed and sugary items are often found.

One of the best ways to maintain a balanced diet is through meal planning and preparation. By planning your meals in advance, you can ensure that your diet includes a variety of nutrients and avoids unhealthy choices. Preparing meals at home allows you to control the ingredients and portion sizes, making it easier to stick to your dietary goals. Batch cooking and prepping meals for the week can save time and reduce the temptation to resort to fast food or processed options.

A balanced diet isn't just about what you eat but also how you distribute your food intake throughout the day. Eating balanced meals at regular intervals helps maintain stable blood sugar levels, provides consistent energy, and prevents overeating. Start your day with a nutrient-rich breakfast, include a balanced mix of proteins, carbs, and fats in your lunch and dinner, and opt for healthy snacks like fruits, nuts, or yoghurt between meals to keep hunger at bay.

Breakfast is often referred to as the most important meal of the day, and for good reason. A balanced breakfast jumpstarts your metabolism, provides essential nutrients after an overnight fast, and sets the tone for healthy eating throughout the day. Include a good mix of protein, healthy fats, and fibre, such as whole-grain toast and a side of fruit, in your breakfast to keep you energised and focused.

Mindful eating is a practice that encourages you to be fully present during meals, paying attention to the flavours, textures, and sensations of your food. By eating slowly and savouring each bite, you're more likely to recognise when you're full, reducing the risk of overeating. Mindful eating also enhances your appreciation for food and helps you make more conscious choices about what and how much you eat. While maintaining a balanced diet is important, it's equally crucial to allow yourself the occasional indulgence. Completely depriving yourself of your favourite treats can lead to cravings and overeating. Instead, practice balance by enjoying indulgent foods in moderation.

Developing Self-Control:

Self-control is a fundamental trait that helps you regulate your emotions, behaviours, and impulses to pursue long-term goals. Developing self-control is not only essential for personal growth but also vital in achieving success in various aspects of life, from health and relationships to career and finances. Let's explore some practical strategies and techniques for cultivating self-control.

Self-control is the ability to make decisions that align with your long-term goals rather than succumbing to immediate temptations. Whether it's resisting the urge to eat unhealthy foods, refraining from procrastination, or avoiding impulsive spending, self-control plays a critical role in helping you make choices that support your overall well-being. By strengthening your self-control, you can improve your decision-making abilities and ensure that your actions align with your values and aspirations. Self-control is closely linked to emotional regulation, which is the ability to manage and constructively respond to your emotions. Developing self-control helps you remain calm and composed in challenging situations, preventing impulsive reactions that may lead to negative outcomes. By practising self-control, you can enhance your emotional resilience, improve your relationships, and navigate stressful situations with greater ease.

One of the foundational techniques for developing self-control is setting clear goals and establishing boundaries. When you have a well-defined goal, it becomes easier to avoid distractions and stay focused on what truly matters. Setting boundaries, such as limiting screen time or avoiding certain environments that trigger impulsive behaviour, can help you maintain control over your actions. By clearly defining your goals and boundaries, you create a structured framework that supports disciplined behaviour. Large, ambitious goals can sometimes feel overwhelming, leading to a loss of self-control when faced with challenges. To counter this, break down your goals into smaller, manageable steps. This approach not only makes your goals more attainable but also helps you build self-control incrementally. Each small achievement reinforces your self-discipline, making it easier to stay committed to your larger objectives.

Delayed gratification is the ability to resist the attraction of immediate rewards in favour of greater rewards in the future. This practice is a powerful tool for developing self-control. By training yourself to wait for a better outcome, you strengthen your ability to manage impulses. For example, if you're tempted to buy something you don't need, practice delaying the purchase for a day or two. The initial desire will fade, and you'll find it easier to make a more rational decision. Mindfulness is a practice that involves being fully present in the moment and observing your thoughts and emotions without judgement. By cultivating mindfulness, you can develop greater self-awareness, which is essential for self-control.

Regular mindfulness practices, such as meditation or deep breathing exercises, help you recognise triggers that lead to impulsive behaviour. By reflecting on your actions and understanding the underlying causes, you can make conscious choices that align with your goals. Positive reinforcement is an effective technique for developing self-control by rewarding yourself for disciplined behaviour. This creates a positive association with self-control, making it easier to repeat disciplined behaviours in the future.

Mental toughness is the ability to persevere through challenges and maintain focus on your goals, even when faced with obstacles. Developing mental toughness involves pushing yourself beyond your comfort zone, embracing challenges, and learning to cope with discomfort. Techniques like visualisation, where you imagine yourself successfully navigating difficult situations, can enhance your mental resilience. By cultivating mental toughness, you increase your capacity for self-control, allowing you to stay committed to your objectives even in the face of adversity.

Holding yourself accountable for your actions is an important component of developing self-control. Self-accountability involves regularly reviewing your progress, acknowledging mistakes, and making necessary adjustments to stay on track. One effective method is to keep a journal where you document your goals, challenges, and successes. By tracking your progress regularly, you create a sense of responsibility and ownership over your actions, which reinforces your commitment to self-control.

Your environment plays a significant role in your ability to exercise self-control. Surround yourself with people, tools, and resources that support your goals and minimise exposure to temporary attractions. For example, if you're trying to eat healthier, stock your pantry with nutritious foods and avoid keeping junk food at home. By creating a supportive environment, you make it easier to practise self-control and maintain disciplined behaviour. Routine and habit formation are powerful strategies for developing self-control. When certain behaviours become habitual, they require less conscious effort, freeing up mental energy for other tasks. Establish routines that align with your goals, such as setting a regular time for exercise, meditation, or productive work. Over time, these habits will become second nature, making it easier to maintain self-control in other areas of your life.

One of the most challenging aspects of self-control is learning to say no, whether it's to yourself or others. However, saying no is an important skill for maintaining discipline and staying focused on your priorities. Practice assertiveness by politely declining offers or invitations that don't align with your goals. By learning to say no, you protect your time and energy, allowing you to channel them into activities that truly matter.

Stress is a common trigger for the loss of self-control, leading to impulsive decisions and unhealthy behaviours. Developing effective stress management techniques, such as exercise, relaxation, or hobbies, can help you maintain self-control even in difficult situations. Regularly practising these techniques reduces the impact of stress on your decision-making process, allowing you to stay calm and focused on your goals.

Willpower, much like a muscle, can be strengthened through regular practice. Engage in small, daily challenges that require self-control, such as resisting the urge to check your phone during work or avoiding unnecessary purchases. Each successful exercise of willpower enhances your overall self-control, making it easier to tackle larger challenges in the future. Developing self-control is a multifaceted process that requires a combination of awareness, discipline, and practice. By setting clear goals, practising delayed gratification, cultivating mindfulness, and creating supportive environments, you can strengthen your ability to regulate your actions and achieve your objectives. Through consistent effort and dedication, you can master the art of self-control and unlock your full potential.

Enhancing Concentration:

Concentration is the ability to direct your mental effort toward a particular task or goal, minimising distractions and maintaining sustained attention. It's a crucial skill for productivity, learning, and achieving success in various aspects of life. Enhancing concentration requires the cultivation of specific practices and strategies that sharpen focus, optimise brain function, and create an environment conducive to deep work.

Just like physical muscles, concentration can be strengthened through regular and deliberate practice. By treating your ability to focus as a skill, you shift your mindset from frustration to empowerment. With this perspective, you'll be more motivated to engage in practices that build concentration and sustain it over longer periods. Concentration isn't just about focus; it's about optimising cognitive processes like memory, problem-solving, and critical thinking. When you enhance your concentration, you improve your brain's ability to process information efficiently, improving your decision-making skills and allowing you to learn more effectively. This cognitive boost can have wide-ranging effects on your productivity and success in both personal and professional realms.

Time management also plays an important role in enhancing concentration. One effective method is time-blocking, where you designate specific periods during the day for focused work. During these blocks, eliminate distractions, set clear goals, and commit to working on one task at a time. Using techniques like the Pomodoro Technique, working for 25 minutes, followed by a 5-minute break, can help maintain high levels of concentration by balancing focused effort with rest. Just as physical exercises strengthen the body, mental exercises can enhance concentration. Practices such as counting backwards in multiples, solving puzzles, or practising mental math can challenge your brain and improve its ability to maintain focus. Another effective exercise is "candle meditation," where you focus on the flame of a candle for several minutes without letting your mind wander. This practice trains your brain to stay locked on a single point of attention.

Prioritising tasks according to their importance can significantly enhance concentration. When you focus on high-priority tasks, you're more likely to give them the attention they deserve. Additionally, breaking down large tasks into smaller, manageable parts can reduce feelings of overwhelm, making it easier to concentrate on each step without getting distracted by the bigger picture.

Environmental factors play a crucial role in your ability to concentrate. Identify and eliminate distractions in your workspace; this might include putting your phone on silent, using noise-cancelling headphones, or setting up a clean, organised desk. Minimising clutter and arranging your space to support focus can significantly enhance your ability to concentrate. Mindfulness techniques, which involve bringing your full attention to the present moment, can be incredibly beneficial for concentration. Engaging in mindfulness meditation, where you focus on your breath or a particular thought, helps train the brain to resist distractions and stay engaged with the task at hand. Regular practice of mindfulness strengthens the neural pathways associated with sustained attention, making it easier to concentrate for longer periods.

While it might seem counterintuitive, taking regular movement breaks can actually improve concentration. Short bursts of physical activity, such as stretching, walking, or doing a few exercises increase blood flow to the brain, which can boost alertness and focus when you return to your tasks. These breaks prevent mental fatigue and help you maintain a high level of concentration throughout the day. Multitasking is a common habit that dilutes concentration and reduces efficiency. Instead, practice single-tasking, where you devote your full attention to one task at a time. This approach allows you to dive deeper into your work, leading to higher-quality outcomes and a more satisfying sense of accomplishment. Over time, single-tasking can significantly enhance your overall ability to concentrate.

Including visual aids, like to-do lists, mind maps, or focus boards, can help keep your concentration on track by providing clear visual reminders of what needs to be done. Similarly, auditory aids like background music or white noise can help by avoiding distracting sounds and creating a consistent auditory environment that supports concentration. Experiment with different types of music or ambient sounds to find what works best for you. Creating a pre-focus ritual can signal to your brain that it's time to concentrate. This could involve a series of actions you take before starting work, such as deep breathing exercises, drinking a glass of water, or reviewing your goals for the session. Over time, this ritual becomes associated with focused work, helping you slip into a state of concentration more quickly and effectively.

While maintaining a balanced diet is essential for physical well-being, certain foods can also support brain health and improve concentration. Omega-3 fatty acids (found in flaxseeds and walnuts), antioxidants (found in berries and leafy greens), and hydration are all key contributors to optimal brain function. By fuelling your body with brain-boosting nutrients, you support sustained focus and cognitive performance.

Keeping a daily journal for recording your concentration levels, distractions, and productivity can be a powerful tool for enhancing focus. By regularly reviewing your entries, you can identify patterns and make adjustments to your environment, habits, or mindset that support better concentration. This reflective practice also reinforces your commitment to improving focus and keeps you accountable to your goals.

Positive emotions can enhance concentration by reducing stress and fostering a mindset of openness and curiosity. Practising gratitude, by taking a few moments each day to reflect on what you're thankful for, can shift your focus away from negativity and distractions. By cultivating a positive outlook, you create a mental environment that supports sustained concentration and engagement with your tasks. Visualisation involves mentally rehearsing the process of staying focused and successfully completing a task. Before starting your work, take a few minutes to visualise yourself concentrating fully, overcoming distractions, and achieving your goal. This mental rehearsal primes your brain for focused work and can significantly enhance your concentration during the actual task.

Enhancing concentration is a process that requires patience and persistence. If you find yourself struggling to focus, practice self-compassion rather than self-criticism. Acknowledge that concentration can fluctuate and focus on opportunities for growth rather than failures. This compassionate approach helps maintain motivation and prevents burnout, making it easier to build and sustain concentration over time.

Building Consistency:

Consistency is a cornerstone of achieving long-term success in any field. It involves maintaining steady effort even when motivation gets low or obstacles arise. Building consistency is about establishing habits and routines that become second nature, allowing you to persist in your goals regardless of external circumstances.

Success is not just the result of one-time efforts or short bursts of activity. Instead, it is the result of consistent actions and decisions that accumulate over time. Whether you're working toward a fitness goal, learning a new skill, or advancing in your career, consistency is what transforms your efforts into lasting achievements. It creates a stable foundation upon which you can build and expand your capabilities. Habits are the building blocks of consistency. When you consistently perform a behaviour over time, it becomes ingrained in your routine, requiring less conscious effort to maintain. This automaticity allows you to sustain progress even when motivation is low, as your habits propel you forward. Understanding the relationship between consistency and habit formation can help you focus on building the right habits that support your long-term goals.

One of the most effective ways to build consistency is to start with small, manageable actions and gradually increase the intensity or complexity over time. For example, if you're trying to develop a consistent exercise routine, begin with short, simple workouts that you can easily fit into your schedule. As you build the habit, gradually increase the duration and intensity of your workouts. This approach prevents burnout and makes it easier to stick with your goals over the long term. Vague goals can lead to inconsistent efforts because they lack direction. To build consistency, set clear, specific, and measurable goals that outline exactly what you want to achieve. Break these goals down into actionable steps and create a timeline for completion. Having a clear roadmap helps you stay focused and consistent in your efforts, as you always know what the next step is and how it fits into your overall plan.

Accountability is also a powerful motivator for consistency. Whether it's sharing your goals with a friend, joining a group with similar objectives, or using a habit-tracking app, having a system that holds you accountable can keep you on track. Regular check-ins with an accountability partner or group provide external motivation and reinforce your commitment to maintaining consistent effort. To build consistency, design your surroundings in a way that encourages the behaviours you want to sustain. This might include placing reminders of your goals in visible locations, organising your workspace to minimise distractions, or creating specific areas for certain activities (e.g., a designated workout space). By aligning your environment with your goals, you create cues that trigger consistent actions.

Rewarding yourself for consistent behaviour can strengthen your commitment and make it easier to maintain. Positive reinforcement, such as celebrating small wins or treating yourself after completing a challenging task, creates a positive association with the behaviour you're trying to sustain. Over time, these rewards can make consistency feel more enjoyable and less like a chore. While routine and discipline are related, the focus here is on using routines to automate your actions. When you establish routines, you reduce the cognitive load required to make decisions, making it easier to maintain consistency. For example, creating a morning routine that includes exercise, goal-setting, and a healthy breakfast can set the tone for a productive day. By sticking to your routine, you build consistency without relying solely on willpower. Consistency is a long-term game that requires patience and persistence. It's important to recognise that progress may be slow at times, and setbacks are a natural part of the journey. By adopting a mindset of patience, you allow yourself to stay the course even when results aren't immediately visible. Persistence, on the other hand, is about continuing to put in effort despite challenges, knowing that consistency will eventually lead to success.

Perfectionism can be a major barrier to consistency. The belief that you need to do something perfectly often leads to procrastination or giving up when things don't go as planned. To build consistency, embrace the idea of "good enough" and focus on making progress rather than perfection. Allow yourself to make mistakes and learn from them, rather than letting them derail your efforts. Monitoring your progress can provide valuable feedback and motivation to stay consistent. Regularly reviewing your progress helps reinforce your commitment and keeps you focused on your long-term goals.

Life is unpredictable, and obstacles are inevitable. Building consistency requires anticipating challenges and developing strategies to overcome them. For example, if you're trying to maintain a consistent exercise routine, plan for potential obstacles like travel, illness, or busy schedules. Having a backup plan, such as a shorter workout or a different activity, can help you stay consistent even when things don't go as planned.

One effective way to build consistency is to "stack" new habits onto existing routines. By anchoring new habits to established routines, you make them easier to remember and more likely to stick. Imagine the satisfaction and success you'll feel when you reach your objectives. This mental rehearsal reinforces your commitment to consistency and keeps you motivated to stay on track. While structure is important for consistency, it's equally important to be flexible when necessary. Aim for a balance between structure and flexibility, and maintain your consistency by adapting your approach when needed, without losing sight of your goals.

Practising Self-Reflection:

Self-reflection is the process of introspection, where you examine your thoughts, feelings, actions, and experiences to gain deeper insight into yourself. It allows you to identify patterns, learn from your mistakes, and align your actions with your values and goals. Unlike self-control, discipline, or routines, self-reflection involves a mindful examination of your inner world to better understand your motivations, desires, and the impact of your behaviour.

Self-reflection provides the clarity required to understand why you think, feel, and act the way you do. It helps you step back from the immediacy of life's demands and observe your experiences from a more detached perspective. This clarity allows you to see situations more objectively, helping you make more informed decisions and avoid being swept away by emotions or impulses. Regular self-reflection allows you to assess your strengths and weaknesses. By recognising areas where you excel and areas where you need improvement, you can develop a more balanced self-awareness. This knowledge is crucial for personal and professional growth, as it enables you to leverage your strengths and work on your weaknesses in a targeted manner.

Through self-reflection, you can identify emotional triggers that influence your behaviour. These triggers are often rooted in past experiences and can lead to automatic responses that may not always serve your best interests. By understanding your emotional triggers, you can develop strategies to manage them more effectively, leading to better emotional regulation and healthier relationships. Self-reflection helps you assess whether your actions align with your core values and beliefs. It's easy to get caught up in the hustle of daily life and lose sight of what truly matters to you. Reflecting on your choices and behaviours allows you to course-correct when necessary, ensuring that you live in a way that is authentic to your values.

Writing down your thoughts and experiences in a journal is a powerful self-reflection technique. Journaling allows you to externalise your internal dialogue, making it easier to analyse and understand your thoughts and feelings. Regular journaling can help you track your progress over time, identify recurring patterns, and gain insights that might be difficult to notice at the moment. Meditation is another effective way to practice self-reflection. Mindful meditation involves focusing on the present moment and observing your thoughts without judgement. This practice can help you become more aware of your mental and emotional states, allowing you to reflect on them with greater clarity.

Developing the habit of asking yourself reflective questions can deepen your self-awareness. Questions such as “What did I learn from today’s experiences?” or “How did I handle challenges, and what could I have done differently?” encourage you to think critically about your actions and their outcomes. These questions can be a part of your daily routine, helping you build a practice of continuous self-improvement.

While self-reflection is an internal process, seeking feedback from others can provide valuable external perspectives. Engaging in honest conversations with trusted friends, family members, or mentors can help you see yourself through their eyes. This feedback can highlight blind spots that you may not have noticed and provide a more well-rounded understanding of your behaviour. A life audit is a more comprehensive form of self-reflection, where you review various aspects of your life, such as career, relationships, health, and personal growth over a set period. By assessing your satisfaction and progress in these areas, you can identify where changes or improvements are needed. Life audits help you maintain a broader perspective on your personal development and ensure that you're moving in the right direction.

Reflecting on what you're grateful for can shift your mindset towards positivity and appreciation. Gratitude reflection involves focusing on the positive aspects of your life, no matter how small, and acknowledging the value they bring. This practice helps counterbalance the tendency to dwell on negative experiences and enhances your overall well-being. Engaging in reflective dialogue with a partner or group can provide deeper insights than solitary reflection. Conversations that encourage self-exploration, such as discussing personal challenges, goals, or philosophical questions, can help you articulate your thoughts more clearly and refine your understanding of yourself. Reflective dialogue also allows you to explore different perspectives, which can enhance your self-reflection process.

Establishing a regular ritual for self-reflection can help make it a consistent part of your life. Whether it's setting aside time each evening to reflect on your day, or dedicating a weekly session to review your progress and goals, creating a structured time for reflection ensures that you prioritise this important practice. Rituals also provide a sense of routine, making it easier to integrate self-reflection into your daily life. For those who find traditional methods of self-reflection challenging, artistic expression can be an alternative way to explore your inner world. Drawing, painting, music, or writing poetry can help you process and reflect on your emotions in a more creative and less structured way. Artistic expression allows you to tap into your subconscious and uncover insights that might be difficult to access through conventional reflection techniques.

Designate a specific space in your home or environment where you can engage in self-reflection without distractions. This space should be comfortable and conducive to introspection, whether it's a quiet corner, a meditation nook, or a peaceful outdoor spot. Having a dedicated space for reflection helps signal to your mind that it's time to pause and think deeply. Consider recording your reflections using audio or video if writing isn't your preferred method.

Speaking your thoughts out loud can help clarify your ideas and emotions. Over time, you can review these recordings to track your growth and identify recurring themes or patterns in your reflections. Experiment with different modalities of self-reflection, such as free writing, guided reflection exercises, or even reflecting through movement (e.g., yoga or walking meditation). Trying various methods can help you discover what works best for you and keep your self-reflection practice fresh and engaging.

Just as you set goals for other areas of your life, set specific goals for your self-reflection practice. For example, you might aim to reflect on a particular area of your life each week or set a goal to uncover a specific insight or realisation. Setting reflection goals helps keep you focused and intentional in your self-reflection efforts. While self-reflection is essential, it's important to balance reflection with action. Use your reflections to inform your decisions and take concrete steps towards your goals. Reflection should not lead to overthinking or paralysis but rather to clearer, more deliberate action. By regularly reflecting and then acting on your insights, you create a cycle of continuous improvement and growth.

Setting Boundaries:

Boundaries are the limits we establish to protect our emotional, physical, and mental health, ensuring that our interactions and environments support our values and needs. Unlike topics such as self-discipline or routine, setting boundaries involves defining and communicating limits to safeguard your personal space, time, and energy.

Boundaries are essential for preserving your sense of self and personal integrity. They help you protect your values, beliefs, and identity by ensuring that you don't compromise them to meet others' expectations or demands. Setting clear boundaries allows you to stay true to yourself and maintain a consistent sense of self-worth and self-respect. Establishing boundaries helps prevent burnout by managing your workload and ensuring that you allocate time for rest and self-care. Without boundaries, you may find yourself overcommitting to tasks or responsibilities, leading to physical and emotional exhaustion. Effective boundary-setting improves communication by clarifying your needs and expectations to others. Boundaries play a vital role in maintaining healthy relationships. They define acceptable behaviour and establish the parameters for mutual respect. By setting boundaries, you prevent others from overstepping their limits and create a more balanced dynamic where both parties feel valued and understood.

Before you can set effective boundaries, it's important to identify your needs and limits. Reflect on areas where you feel overwhelmed, uncomfortable, or disrespected. Clear and assertive communication is key to setting boundaries. Use "I" statements to express your needs and limits without placing blame or sounding accusatory. For example, instead of saying, "You always interrupt me," say, "I need uninterrupted time to complete my work." Consistency is crucial when setting boundaries. Boundaries are essential for effective time management. Set limits on how much time you spend on various activities, such as work, social engagements, or leisure. Setting boundaries can sometimes lead to feelings of guilt or discomfort, especially if you're not used to asserting your needs. Practice self-compassion by acknowledging that setting boundaries is a healthy and necessary practice for your well-being. Physical boundaries involve defining your personal space and respecting others' physical space. Communicate your comfort levels regarding physical contact and proximity in various situations. Emotional boundaries involve protecting your emotional well-being by managing how much you allow others to affect your emotions. Set limits on how much emotional energy you invest in relationships or situations that drain you. When someone crosses your boundaries, address the violation promptly and assertively.

In today's digital age, setting boundaries with technology is essential for maintaining work-life balance and personal well-being. Define limits on your use of devices, social media, and email to avoid constant connectivity and potential stress. For example, establish specific times for checking emails and avoid using devices during designated relaxation periods. Boundaries may need to be reviewed and adjusted as your life circumstances change. Regular reviews ensure that your boundaries continue to serve your needs and support your well-being.

Create a structured plan for setting and maintaining boundaries. Outline specific boundaries you want to establish in different areas of your life, such as work, relationships, and personal time. Include strategies for communicating and enforcing these boundaries. A written plan helps you stay organised and focused on maintaining your limits. Practice setting boundaries through role-playing scenarios with a trusted friend or mentor. Role-playing helps you rehearse how to communicate your boundaries effectively and handle potential challenges. Regularly reflect on your experiences with setting and maintaining boundaries. Identify what has worked well and where you've faced challenges. If setting boundaries feels challenging, seek support from a counsellor, therapist, or coach. Professional guidance can help you develop effective boundary-setting skills and address any underlying issues.

Personal Growth:

Personal growth is an ongoing process of self-improvement and development that encompasses various aspects of your life. It involves expanding your abilities, understanding yourself better, and striving to achieve your fullest potential. Unlike topics such as routine or boundaries, personal growth is a journey that integrates your physical, emotional, mental, and spiritual dimensions, which requires intentional effort and a commitment to continuous learning and self-discovery.

Personal growth begins with self-discovery, which involves exploring your values, passions, strengths, and weaknesses. Understanding who you are and what drives you provides a solid foundation for setting meaningful goals and making informed decisions. Self-discovery helps you align your actions with your true self, fostering a sense of authenticity and fulfilment. Growth often requires stepping out of your comfort zone and facing new challenges. By pushing beyond familiar boundaries, you expose yourself to new experiences and opportunities for learning. Expanding your comfort zone encourages resilience, adaptability, and the development of new skills, all of which contribute to personal growth.

Continuously seeking knowledge and skills through reading, courses, workshops, or new experiences broadens your perspective and enhances your capabilities. Embracing a learning mindset helps you stay curious, open-minded, and adaptable to change. Personal growth also involves developing resilience by facing difficulties head-on and learning from them. Building resilience equips you with the mental strength to navigate obstacles and maintain a positive outlook, even in the face of adversity.

Emotional intelligence (EI) plays a significant role in personal growth. It involves understanding and managing your own emotions, as well as empathising with others. Cultivating EI enhances your interpersonal relationships, communication skills, and overall emotional well-being, contributing to a more balanced and fulfilling life. Personal growth is supported by the development of positive habits that align with your goals and values. Habits such as regular exercise, mindful meditation, or effective time management contribute to your overall well-being and productivity.

Developing a personal development plan involves setting specific, measurable, and time-bound goals for your growth. Outline the steps you need to take to achieve these goals and track your progress regularly. A well-structured plan provides clarity and direction, helping you stay focused and motivated. By acknowledging that growth is a gradual process and accepting your imperfections, you foster a positive and supportive internal environment. Self-compassion enhances your resilience and encourages a more balanced approach to growth. Actively seek out new experiences that challenge and inspire you. Whether it's travelling to a new destination, trying a new hobby, or taking on a new project, exposing yourself to diverse experiences broadens your horizons and promotes personal growth. Embrace opportunities to learn and grow from different contexts and perspectives.

Surround yourself with people who share your values and aspirations and who can provide guidance and accountability. Cultivate a growth mindset, which is the belief that abilities and intelligence can be developed through effort and learning. Embracing a growth mindset helps you view challenges as opportunities for growth rather than obstacles. This mindset encourages perseverance, curiosity, and a willingness to embrace new learning experiences. Join communities or groups focused on personal growth and development. Engaging with others who share similar goals and interests provides opportunities for learning, networking, and support. Being part of a personal growth community helps you stay motivated, gain new insights, and connect with like-minded individuals.

Limiting Distractions:

Limiting distractions is essential for maintaining focus and maximising productivity in both personal and professional settings. Distractions can derail your progress, reduce the quality of your work, and increase stress. By implementing strategies to minimise distractions, you can create an environment conducive to concentration and effective task management.

Distractions can significantly lower your efficiency by interrupting your workflow and increasing the time needed to complete tasks. Frequent interruptions force you to shift your attention, leading to decreased productivity and longer completion times. Limiting distractions helps streamline your focus and enhances your ability to work efficiently. Constant interruptions and distractions can elevate stress levels by creating a sense of urgency and overwhelming your cognitive load. Managing distractions helps reduce stress by allowing you to maintain a steady workflow and manage your workload more effectively. When distractions are prevalent, the quality of your work can suffer. Interruptions can lead to errors, incomplete tasks, and reduced attention to detail. By minimising distractions, you can improve the quality of your work and ensure that tasks are completed with greater accuracy and thoroughness. Distractions can impair your ability to retain and process information. Constant interruptions disrupt cognitive processes, making it challenging to focus and remember key details. Limiting distractions helps enhance your memory and learning capabilities by allowing you to concentrate on one task at a time.

Create a dedicated workspace that is free from potential distractions. Choose a quiet location where you can work without interruptions from noise, people, or other external factors. Ensure that your workspace is organised and clutter-free to maintain focus and reduce visual distractions. Allocate specific time blocks for focused work and commit to working during these periods without interruptions. You can also use the Pomodoro Technique, as mentioned earlier. Digital distractions, such as notifications from social media, emails, or messaging apps, can disrupt your focus. Turn off non-essential notifications and set specific times to check your email or social media accounts. Consider using website blockers or productivity apps to restrict access to distracting websites during work periods. Communicate your need for focused work time to colleagues, family members, or roommates. Set clear boundaries regarding when you are available for interruptions and when you need uninterrupted work time. Establishing these boundaries helps others respect your focus and minimises potential distractions.

If noise is a distraction in your environment, consider using noise-cancelling headphones or white noise machines. These tools can help mask background noise and create a more conducive environment for concentration. Choose audio options that enhance your focus, such as instrumental music or nature sounds.

The two-minute rule involves addressing tasks that can be completed in two minutes immediately. By handling quick tasks promptly, you prevent them from becoming distractions later. This approach helps you manage small tasks efficiently and keeps them from interfering with your focused work periods. Multitasking can lead to decreased focus and increased errors. Instead of juggling multiple tasks simultaneously, concentrate on completing one task at a time. Use techniques like task batching to group similar tasks together and complete them sequentially. This approach enhances focus and improves overall productivity.

Identify environments or situations that tend to induce distractions and limit your access to them during work periods. For example, if working in a coffee shop is distracting, consider working in a quieter location to mitigate the impact of the environment. Use visual reminders or cues to keep your focus on tasks and minimise distractions. Place reminders or motivational quotes in your workspace to reinforce your commitment to staying focused. Visual reminders help keep your goals and priorities in view, enhancing your concentration and motivation.

Establish a routine for transitioning between tasks or work periods to minimise the impact of distractions. Create a structured process for shifting your focus from one task to another, such as taking a brief pause or using a transition activity. This routine helps you manage distractions and maintain a smooth workflow.

Embracing Responsibilities:

Taking responsibility is a fundamental aspect of personal and professional development. Embracing ownership of your duties and obligations not only enhances your effectiveness but also fosters a sense of purpose and accountability. It involves understanding the importance of your roles, proactively managing your commitments, and cultivating a mindset that supports growth and achievement.

Embracing responsibilities instils a sense of accountability, which is important for personal and professional growth. When you take ownership of your tasks and commitments, you hold yourself accountable for their outcomes. This sense of responsibility drives you to complete tasks effectively and meet expectations, reinforcing your reliability and trustworthiness. Consistently fulfilling your responsibilities builds trust and credibility with others. Whether in personal relationships, professional settings, or community involvement, demonstrating reliability and competence enhances your reputation. Others are more likely to rely on and support you when they see that you can be trusted to handle responsibilities effectively.

Embracing responsibilities contributes to personal growth by challenging you to develop new skills, manage your time effectively, and navigate complex situations. Taking on diverse responsibilities exposes you to different experiences and opportunities for learning, helping you expand your capabilities and achieve personal development goals. Responsibilities often align with your values, goals, and aspirations. By embracing your roles and duties, you create a sense of purpose and direction in your life. Understanding how your responsibilities contribute to a larger purpose or mission helps you stay motivated and focused on achieving your objectives.

Handling responsibilities involves addressing challenges and finding solutions to problems. Embracing your roles encourages you to develop problem-solving skills and think critically. By tackling obstacles and finding effective solutions, you enhance your ability to manage complex situations and achieve desired outcomes.

Use goal-setting techniques, such as SMART (Specific, Measurable, Achievable, Relevant, Time-bound) goals, to clarify your responsibilities. Create a plan of action to manage your responsibilities efficiently. Break down tasks into manageable steps, establish deadlines, and prioritise your commitments. A structured plan helps you stay organised and ensures that you address each responsibility on time. Effective communication is key to embracing responsibilities. Clearly communicate your commitments, progress, and any challenges you encounter to relevant stakeholders. Open and transparent communication fosters collaboration, builds trust, and ensures that everyone is aligned with expectations and responsibilities.

Adopt a proactive mindset by anticipating potential challenges and taking the initiative to address them. Instead of waiting for problems to arise, proactively identify opportunities for improvement and take action to resolve issues. A proactive approach enhances your ability to manage responsibilities and achieve successful outcomes.

Time management is essential for handling multiple responsibilities effectively. Use time management techniques, such as creating a daily schedule, setting priorities, and avoiding procrastination, to ensure that you allocate sufficient time to each responsibility. When embracing responsibilities, seek support and resources as needed. Whether it's guidance from a mentor, assistance from colleagues, or access to tools and resources, leveraging support can help you manage your responsibilities more effectively. Don't hesitate to ask for help or utilise available resources to achieve your goals.

Self-discipline is crucial for staying focused and committed to your responsibilities. Develop habits that reinforce your ability to manage your tasks and avoid distractions. Self-discipline helps you maintain consistency, follow through on commitments, and achieve your objectives. Learning from both successes and challenges helps you refine your approach to managing responsibilities and enhances your overall effectiveness.

While embracing responsibilities is important, it's also essential to balance them with self-care. Ensure that you allocate time for rest, relaxation, and personal well-being. Maintaining a healthy balance helps you manage stress, prevent burnout, and sustain your ability to handle responsibilities effectively. Regularly evaluate your approach to managing responsibilities and make adjustments as needed. A growth mindset encourages you to embrace new responsibilities and pursue continuous improvement.

Perseverance:

Perseverance is the determination to continue pursuing a goal despite obstacles and setbacks. It plays a crucial role in personal and professional success, as it enables individuals to overcome difficulties, maintain motivation, and ultimately achieve their objectives.

Perseverance is essential for navigating challenges and setbacks that inevitably arise on the path to achieving goals. It allows you to face difficulties head-on, adapt to changing circumstances, and persist in the face of obstacles. By embracing perseverance, you can overcome adversity and continue progressing toward your objectives. Perseverance helps sustain motivation over time, even when progress is slow or obstacles arise. By remaining focused on your goals and consistently working toward them, you reinforce your commitment and motivation. This sustained effort helps you achieve milestones and maintain momentum throughout your journey.

Perseverance often involves addressing and solving problems that arise during the pursuit of goals. By persistently tackling challenges and seeking solutions, you enhance your problem-solving skills and develop creative approaches to overcoming obstacles. Success is rarely instantaneous and often requires sustained effort and perseverance. By maintaining a long-term perspective and continuing to work toward your goals despite setbacks, you increase your chances of achieving long-term success. Perseverance ensures that you stay committed to your objectives and see them through to completion.

Accept failure as a natural part of the journey toward success. Instead of viewing failure as a defeat, use it as an opportunity to learn and grow. Analyse what went wrong, identify areas for improvement, and adjust your approach accordingly. This involves acknowledging your efforts, recognising that setbacks are part of the process, and avoiding self-criticism. This helps you maintain a positive mindset and persevere through difficulties. Cultivate a positive attitude to enhance your ability to persevere. A positive attitude helps you stay motivated and resilient, making it easier to overcome challenges and continue pursuing your goals.

Be open to adjusting your approach and strategies as needed. Flexibility and adaptability allow you to navigate changes and unforeseen challenges effectively. Embracing adaptability ensures that you can persevere through evolving circumstances and continue progressing toward your objectives. Commit to making consistent, incremental progress each day. Persistence in daily efforts helps you build momentum and maintain focus on your goals. By consistently working toward your objectives, you reinforce your perseverance and increase your chances of success. Imagine yourself achieving your goals.

Look to role models who have demonstrated perseverance in their journeys. Learning about the experiences and strategies of successful individuals can provide valuable insights and inspiration. Role models can serve as examples of how perseverance leads to success and motivates you to continue pursuing your goals. Identify and implement coping strategies to manage stress and challenges effectively. Techniques such as problem-solving approaches can help you stay focused and resilient during difficult times. By setting clear goals, developing a growth mindset, and creating a supportive environment, you can strengthen your ability to persevere.

Overcoming Procrastination:

Procrastination, the act of postponing tasks, can undermine productivity and hinder progress. To effectively address procrastination, it's important to explore unique strategies that target various aspects of behaviour and mindset.

The "5-Second Rule," popularised by Mel Robbins, is a simple yet effective technique to counteract procrastination. The principle is to take action within five seconds of having the impulse to do something. This short time frame minimises the opportunity for your brain to rationalise delaying the task. By immediately taking action, you overcome the inertia that fuels procrastination and initiate momentum toward completing the task.

A behavioural contract is a formal agreement between yourself and a partner that outlines specific tasks, deadlines, and consequences. This contract can include rewards for completing tasks or penalties for failing to meet deadlines. The structured nature of a behavioural contract creates a sense of obligation and accountability, encouraging timely action and reducing procrastination.

The "Eat That Frog" technique, based on Brian Tracy's book, involves tackling your most challenging or least appealing task first thing in the day. By prioritising and completing this "frog," you address the task you've been avoiding and set a positive tone for the rest of the day. This technique leverages the satisfaction of completing a difficult task to build momentum and reduce procrastination.

A procrastination journal is a dedicated log where you record instances of procrastination, including the reasons, feelings, and specific tasks involved. Regularly reviewing your journal helps identify patterns and triggers related to procrastination. This self-awareness allows you to address underlying issues and develop targeted strategies to overcome procrastination.

You can also implement gamification techniques. Gamification involves applying game-like elements to non-game contexts to increase engagement and motivation. Create a reward system where you earn points, badges, or other incentives for completing tasks. You can use apps or create your system that makes task completion more engaging and enjoyable. Gamification taps into intrinsic motivation and makes overcoming procrastination a more dynamic process.

The "Two-Minute Action Rule" suggests that if a task can be completed in two minutes or less, do it immediately. This approach prevents small tasks from accumulating and becoming overwhelming. By addressing quick tasks promptly, you maintain momentum and prevent procrastination from escalating. Arrange your workspace or living area with visual reminders, such as sticky notes, task lists, or motivational quotes. These cues serve as constant reminders and prompts to engage in productive activities, minimising the likelihood of procrastination.

Task sequencing involves organising tasks in a specific order to build momentum and facilitate progress. Start with a task that is relatively easy or enjoyable, followed by more challenging or less appealing tasks. This approach leverages the sense of accomplishment from completing initial tasks to make subsequent tasks feel more manageable and reduce procrastination.

Behavioural therapy techniques, such as Cognitive Behavioural Therapy (CBT), can help address procrastination by changing negative thought patterns and behaviours. Techniques such as cognitive restructuring, where you challenge and reframe unproductive thoughts, and behavioural activation, where you gradually increase engagement in tasks, can be effective in overcoming procrastination.

Procrastination can sometimes be linked to stress or anxiety. Progressive muscle relaxation (PMR) is a technique that involves tensing and then relaxing different muscle groups to reduce stress. By practising PMR before tackling tasks, you can alleviate anxiety and create a more relaxed state conducive to productivity.

An accountability chart is a visual tool that tracks your progress on various tasks or projects. Create a chart with specific tasks, deadlines, and progress indicators. Regularly updating the chart and reviewing your progress helps maintain focus and provides a tangible representation of your achievements, encouraging timely action and reducing procrastination.

Time-restricted work sessions involve setting a strict, short period (e.g. 15 or 30 minutes) dedicated solely to a specific task. During this time, focus exclusively on the task without interruptions. The time restriction creates a sense of urgency and helps overcome procrastination by breaking tasks into manageable, focused intervals.

Create a visual progress tracker, such as a progress bar or achievement board, to represent your progress on tasks or projects. Visual representations of progress provide a sense of accomplishment and motivation, making it easier to stay focused and overcome procrastination. These techniques will help you overcome procrastination.

Practising Gratitude and Appreciation:

It involves recognising and acknowledging the positive aspects of life, which can significantly enhance overall well-being and foster a more positive outlook. Unique strategies for incorporating gratitude and appreciation into daily life can lead to greater happiness and increased resilience.

A gratitude jar is a tangible method for practising daily appreciation. Keep a jar and small pieces of paper handy. Each day, write down something you're grateful for or an act of kindness you've experienced. Regularly review the notes to reflect on positive moments and cultivate a sense of appreciation for the good things in your life. Include gratitude in your physical exercise routine by taking "gratitude walks." During these walks, focus on acknowledging and appreciating the natural beauty around you and the positive aspects of your life. Use this time to reflect on what you're thankful for, fostering a sense of connection and mindfulness.

Create personal or family rituals dedicated to expressing appreciation. This could be a weekly dinner where everyone shares something they're grateful for or a monthly gathering where you reflect on positive experiences and achievements. Rituals help embed gratitude into your routine and strengthen relationships.

Practice gratitude visualisation by spending a few minutes each day visualising moments or experiences you're thankful for. Close your eyes and vividly imagine the positive details of these experiences, focusing on the feelings of gratitude they evoke. Visualisation helps reinforce positive emotions and enhances your sense of appreciation.

Write heartfelt gratitude letters to people who have positively impacted your life. Take the time to express your appreciation in detail, acknowledging their influence and the specific ways they have made a difference. Sending these letters, or even just writing them, fosters a deeper connection and allows you to fully acknowledge and appreciate others.

Create a visual "gratitude map" to explore and document various aspects of your life that you are thankful for. Use charts, diagrams, or mind maps to categorise different areas, such as relationships, achievements, or experiences. This visual representation helps you recognise the breadth of things you appreciate and provides a comprehensive view of your gratitude.

Include gratitude affirmations in your daily routine. Craft positive statements that focus on what you're grateful for, such as "I am thankful for my supportive friends" or "I appreciate the opportunities that come my way." Repeat these affirmations regularly to reinforce a grateful mindset and integrate appreciation into your daily thought patterns.

Create a gratitude and appreciation calendar where each day includes a prompt or activity related to expressing gratitude. This could involve writing down a specific thing you're thankful for, acknowledging a person who has made a difference, or reflecting on a positive experience. A calendar provides a structured way to incorporate gratitude into your daily life.

Include appreciation in your daily interactions by making a conscious effort to acknowledge and thank others. Practice expressing genuine appreciation for their efforts, kindness, or positive qualities. Small, regular gestures of gratitude in interactions foster a culture of appreciation and strengthen relationships.

Engage in creative art projects that reflect your gratitude. This could include creating a gratitude collage, painting, or crafting visual representations of things you appreciate. Artistic expression provides a unique way to channel your feelings of gratitude and create tangible reminders of what you value.

Perform acts of service as a form of gratitude practice. Volunteer your time, offer help to others, or engage in community service as a way to express your appreciation for the positive aspects of your life. Acts of service not only benefit others but also reinforce your sense of gratitude and fulfilment.

Include a nightly gratitude reflection as part of your bedtime routine. Spend a few minutes before sleep reflecting on the positive aspects of your day, the things you're grateful for, and moments of appreciation. These practices help you end the day on a positive note and reinforce a grateful mindset.

Showing Compassion:

Showing compassion involves understanding and empathising with others' experiences and emotions, and taking actions to alleviate their suffering or support their well-being. Cultivating compassion can enhance personal relationships and create a positive impact in your community.

Engage in compassionate listening, which goes beyond active listening to truly empathise with the speaker's emotions and experiences. Practice reflective listening by summarising what the other person has shared and validating their feelings. Avoid interrupting or offering immediate solutions; instead, focus on providing a safe space for them to express themselves fully. Include compassion-based meditation into your routine, such as Loving-Kindness Meditation (Metta). This practice involves focusing on sending positive wishes and kind thoughts to yourself, loved ones, and even people you may have conflicts with. By regularly engaging in this meditation, you can enhance your capacity for empathy and compassion towards others.

Perform acts of service with a focus on compassion. Identify specific needs in your community or among your friends and family and offer your help in meaningful ways. This could involve volunteering, organising support for someone in need, or simply offering practical assistance. Acts of service demonstrate a genuine commitment to alleviating others' difficulties. Use empathy mapping as a tool to deepen your understanding of others' experiences. Create a visual map that includes aspects such as what someone is thinking, feeling, saying, and doing.

Share stories of compassion and kindness to inspire others and foster a culture of empathy. Whether through social media, community events, or personal conversations, recounting experiences where compassion made a difference can motivate others to act with similar kindness and understanding. Include random acts of kindness in your daily routine. These spontaneous gestures can include paying for someone's coffee, leaving a kind note for a colleague, or offering a helping hand to a stranger. Such acts of kindness, performed without the expectation of return, foster a sense of compassion and connection in your interactions.

Engage in exercises designed to build empathy and understanding. For example, role-playing activities where you step into someone else's shoes and experience their perspective can deepen your emotional connection and empathy. Enhance your capacity for compassion by participating in cultural sensitivity training. Attend or organise workshops focused on compassionate communication techniques. These workshops teach skills such as nonviolent communication, empathetic listening, and conflict resolution.

Summary:

In this chapter, we explored the concept of self-discipline, discussing practices that foster personal growth and success. We began by emphasising the importance of establishing a routine and rising early, which sets a proactive tone for the day and enhances productivity. Regular exercise and a balanced diet were highlighted as crucial for maintaining physical and mental well-being, supporting sustained focus and energy.

The chapter also covered strategies for developing self-control, enhancing concentration, and building consistency in daily habits. Self-reflection was discussed as a means to assess progress and reinforce discipline while setting boundaries and embracing responsibilities were identified as key to balancing work and personal life. Overcoming procrastination and limiting distractions were addressed as practical steps to achieving goals, alongside the benefits of perseverance and a mindset of gratitude.

Finally, we underscored the importance of compassion towards oneself and others, integrating empathy into disciplined behaviour for a balanced and fulfilling life. Building on our exploration of self-discipline, the next chapter delves into the concept of physical purity, examining how maintaining a healthy body through mindful practices and habits contributes to overall well-being and discipline.

Chapter 2 – Purity

Source: worldpranichealing.com

"One man who has purified himself thoroughly accomplishes more than a regiment of preachers. Out of purity and silence comes the word of power."

–Swami Vivekananda

This quote by Swami Vivekananda expresses the power of personal purity and inner strength. A pure person can achieve more than many who merely talk about good deeds. True power and influence come from purity of thought, action, and a calm, focused mind. When someone is pure, their words and actions carry a great impact, far beyond what others can achieve through mere preaching. With this purity, one can attain true power and effectiveness, making their efforts more meaningful and far-reaching.

Practising cleanliness:

Practising cleanliness is a fundamental step toward achieving physical purity and cultivating a disciplined life. Cleanliness is not just about maintaining an outward appearance; it reflects your inner state of mind and commitment to living a pure and mindful life. The habit of cleanliness forms the foundation for self-discipline, helping you stay organised, focused, and in harmony with your surroundings. The importance of cleanliness begins with the body. Regular bathing and personal hygiene are essential practices. Keeping the body clean not only prevents illness but also refreshes the mind and uplifts the spirit. When you take care of your body, you show respect for yourself and the life you have been given. Cleanliness helps to purify the body and creates a positive state of mind, preparing you for your daily tasks.

Maintaining cleanliness extends beyond personal hygiene to your living space. A clean environment directly impacts your mental and emotional state. When your surroundings are cluttered or dirty, it can create a sense of chaos and disorganisation in your mind. It becomes easier to focus, make decisions, and find peace in a tidy environment. Keeping your home, workspace, and personal belongings in order is an act of self-discipline that reinforces your commitment to a pure and mindful life.

Cleanliness should be practised in your actions and speech. Purity is not just about the body; it also involves your behaviour. Speak with kindness and truthfulness, and avoid using harsh or negative words. Your words have power, and practising cleanliness in speech means being mindful of how your words affect others and yourself. Clean actions, free from deceit and harmful intent, contribute to a life of integrity and righteousness. Developing the habit of cleanliness also means being conscious of the food you eat and the air you breathe. Choose fresh, nutritious foods that nourish your body and avoid substances that harm it. Cleanse your body from within by drinking plenty of water and avoiding unhealthy substances.

Practising cleanliness is an approach that encompasses every aspect of your life (your body, mind, environment, and actions). It is a daily practice that requires effort and awareness but yields profound benefits. By cultivating cleanliness in all areas of your life, you purify yourself physically and create a foundation for spiritual growth and self-discipline. Cleanliness is a virtue that radiates outward, influencing not only your well-being but also the world around you.

Eat Well:

Eating good food is not just about nutrition; it is a practice that aligns with the principles of purity, serving as a bridge between physical well-being and spiritual growth. What you consume directly impacts your body, mind, and soul. By choosing good food, you nourish your entire being and support your journey towards living a disciplined and purposeful life.

Good food begins with the intention behind your choices. When you approach eating with mindfulness, you recognise that food is not merely fuel but a gift from nature that sustains you. Eating with gratitude and awareness transforms a simple meal into an act of reverence. It's important to choose foods that are pure, natural, and unprocessed. Fresh fruits, vegetables, whole grains, and nuts are examples of good food that come directly from nature, untouched by artificial chemicals and additives. These foods provide the vital energy your body needs to function at its best.

Another important aspect of eating good food is being mindful of where your food comes from. Supporting local farmers and choosing organic produce whenever possible ensures that you are consuming food that is grown with care and without harmful pesticides. This practice not only benefits your health but also promotes a sustainable and harmonious relationship with the environment. It is a way of respecting the resources that sustain you. Portion control is also key to eating good food. Overindulgence, even in healthy foods, can lead to imbalance and sluggishness. Moderation is a form of self-discipline that helps you maintain physical purity. By listening to your body's needs and eating in moderation, you prevent overeating and ensure that your body remains in a state of balance. Eating should be a mindful act, where you focus on the quality of the food and how it nourishes you, rather than simply filling yourself up.

More than what you eat, how you eat matters. Eating in a calm and peaceful environment, free from distractions, allows you to fully appreciate your food and its benefits. Chewing slowly and thoroughly helps with digestion and allows your body to absorb nutrients more effectively. When you eat mindfully, you also become more attuned to your body's signals of hunger and fullness, preventing overeating and promoting overall well-being. Avoiding harmful substances such as excessive sugar, processed foods, and junk food is essential. These types of foods may satisfy cravings temporarily, but they deplete your energy and cloud your mind. Instead, focus on foods that uplift your body and spirit, supporting you in your quest for purity and self-discipline. Eating good food is an integral part of physical purity. It is about making conscious choices that nourish your body, respect the earth, and support your spiritual journey. By eating good food, you cultivate a sense of harmony within yourself and with the world around you.

Detoxify Yourself:

Detoxifying yourself is not just about cleansing your body from impurities; it's about creating a fresh start, both physically and mentally. By removing toxins from your body, you pave the way for clarity, vitality, and a deeper connection with your inner self.

The first step in detoxifying yourself is recognising the importance of what you allow into your body. Everything you consume has an impact (whether it's food, drinks, or even the air you breathe). To purify yourself, begin by eliminating substances that can harm your body. Avoid processed foods, sugary drinks, alcohol, and any other substances that introduce toxins into your system. Instead, focus on consuming natural, whole foods that support your body's ability to heal and cleanse itself. Fresh fruits, vegetables, and plenty of water are key components of a detoxifying diet.

Hydration plays a crucial role in the detoxification process. Water is nature's best cleanser. Drinking plenty of water throughout the day helps flush out toxins from your system keeps your organs functioning optimally and improves your skin's health. Herbal teas and natural juices can also support detoxification, offering additional nutrients that aid in the cleansing process.

Fasting, practised with mindfulness, is another powerful way to detoxify the body. By giving your digestive system a break, you allow your body to focus on cleansing itself rather than constantly processing food. A simple fast, even for a few hours or a day, can have profound effects on your physical and mental well-being. During fasting, it's important to maintain a calm state of mind, as stress can counteract the benefits of detoxification.

Including regular physical activity is vital for detoxifying yourself. Exercise helps to stimulate circulation, which in turn encourages the removal of toxins through sweat and improved lymphatic flow. Whether it's a brisk walk, yoga, or more intense physical activity, movement aids your body's natural detox processes and enhances your overall vitality.

Breathing exercises, such as deep breathing or pranayama, can also aid in detoxification. By consciously breathing deeply, you help to oxygenate your blood, release toxins from your lungs, and promote a sense of calm and clarity. Breathing deeply can also help to clear your mind, making it easier to let go of negative thoughts and habits that may be weighing you down. Detoxification is not just a physical process but a mental one as well. Purifying your mind from stress, anger, and resentment can create space for positivity and growth. Meditation, journaling, or simply spending time in nature can help clear your mind and contribute to the detoxification process.

Maintain a Clean Living Space:

A clean living space reflects the state of your mind and spirit, fostering clarity, peace, and positive energy. It benefits not only your physical well-being but also nurtures your mental and emotional health, creating a harmonious environment where you can thrive.

The first step towards maintaining a clean living space is recognising that your environment is an extension of yourself. Just as you strive to purify your body and mind, your living space should be treated with the same care and respect. Regular cleaning and decluttering help remove negative energy, reduce stress, and promote a sense of order and calm.

Start by establishing a routine for cleaning your living space. Consistency is key. Whether it's daily tasks like sweeping, wiping surfaces, and organising items, or weekly deep cleaning sessions, maintaining a schedule ensures that cleanliness becomes a habit rather than a chore. Break tasks into manageable portions to avoid feeling overwhelmed. Small, consistent efforts lead to long-lasting results. Decluttering is an essential part of this process. Often, we accumulate items that no longer serve us, both physically and mentally. Holding on to unnecessary possessions can create stagnation in our lives. Ask yourself if each item in your space adds value to your life. If it doesn't, it might be time to let it go.

It's important to focus on the energy within your space. Negative emotions, stress, and chaos can accumulate in your environment, just as dirt and dust can. Create a positive atmosphere by introducing elements that inspire peace and purity. This could be as simple as letting in natural light, adding plants, or creating a designated space for meditation and reflection. A clean space with positive energy nurtures your soul and keeps you connected to your higher purpose. Maintaining a clean living space also extends to the people you allow into it. Surround yourself with individuals who uplift and inspire you. Just as you cleanse your physical space, be mindful of the emotional and mental energy that others bring into your home. Cultivating an environment of positivity and support is essential for overall well-being.

Wear Clean Clothes:

When you dress in clean, well-maintained attire, you honour both your body and your mind. Clean clothes are not merely about appearance; they represent a commitment to living with dignity, mindfulness, and inner cleanliness. The act of wearing clean clothes begins with the awareness that your external appearance is a reflection of your inner state. Just as you cleanse your body, you should also keep your clothing free of dirt, stains, and unpleasant odours. Cleanliness in dress signals to yourself and others that you value order and harmony in your life. This simple practice can uplift your mood, increase your confidence, and influence how others perceive you.

Maintaining clean clothes requires mindful attention to your laundry routine. Make it a habit to wash your clothes regularly, using natural detergents that are gentle on your skin and the environment. Pay attention to the fabrics you choose to wear. Natural fibres like cotton, linen, and wool breathe better and often feel more comfortable on the skin.

This mindful approach to caring for your clothing ensures that you are not only keeping them clean but also maintaining their quality over time. In addition to cleanliness, consider simplicity in your clothing choices. Wearing clothes that are simple, comfortable, and suitable for your activities helps you stay focused and reduces distractions. When your clothing is comfortable and appropriate, you can move through your day with ease and grace. This practice of simplicity in dress aligns with the broader concept of purity.

It is also important to recognise the connection between clean clothing and your surroundings. Wearing clean clothes fosters a sense of order and respect in all areas of your life. Just as you would keep your living space clean and organised, your clothing should reflect that same level of care. By maintaining cleanliness in your dress, you are reinforcing the values of discipline and purity in your daily actions.

Furthermore, clean clothing has a direct impact on your physical health. It prevents the buildup of bacteria and sweat that can lead to skin irritations and infections. This simple act of self-care is a way to protect your body and maintain overall well-being. Wearing clean clothes is a practice that cultivates self-respect, discipline, and a sense of purpose. It reminds you that purity is not just about your internal state, but also about how you present yourself to the world. You create a positive and pure environment around you, setting the tone for a balanced and meaningful life.

Eliminate Negative Habits:

Negative habits are behaviours that drain your energy, harm your body, and cloud your mind. These habits can range from unhealthy eating patterns to lack of exercise, excessive screen time, or any routine that does not contribute to your well-being. To purify yourself physically, you must recognise these habits and work consistently to remove them from your life.

The first step in eliminating negative habits is self-awareness. You need to take a close look at your daily routines and identify behaviours that are holding you back. This requires honesty and reflection. Ask yourself: What habits make me feel sluggish or unmotivated? What behaviours are detrimental to my health? Once you have identified these negative patterns, you can begin the process of change. Change starts with small, consistent efforts. Trying to eliminate a habit overnight is often unrealistic and can lead to frustration. Instead, focus on gradually reducing the habit. For example, if you tend to overeat unhealthy snacks, start by replacing one unhealthy snack with a healthier option. If you spend too much time on your phone or computer, set specific time limits for screen use. These small adjustments, when practised regularly, lead to significant changes over time.

It's essential to replace negative habits with positive ones. The void left by a removed habit needs to be filled with something constructive, or you may find yourself slipping back into old patterns. For example, if you are trying to cut down on excessive screen time, replace it with reading, physical exercise, or any productive activity that benefits your mind and body. This way, you're not just eliminating the bad habit, but also cultivating a new, positive one.

Support and accountability can also play a significant role in overcoming negative habits. Share your goals with a friend or family member who can encourage you and hold you accountable. Sometimes, discussing your struggles and victories with someone else provides the motivation you need to keep going. Mindfulness is another powerful tool. Being present in the moment allows you to recognise when a negative habit is about to take hold. When you are aware, you can make a conscious choice to resist the habit and choose a better path.

Be patient with yourself. Eliminating negative habits is not an easy process, and setbacks are natural. What matters most is your commitment to progress. Each small victory, no matter how insignificant it may seem, is a step toward a purer, healthier, and more disciplined life.

Practice Non-violence:

Non-violence begins in the mind. Often, violence manifests from negative thoughts, anger, and frustration. Therefore, it is essential to purify your thoughts by nurturing kindness, compassion, and understanding. When you train your mind to think positively, you reduce the chances of engaging in harmful actions or speech. Start by being aware of your thoughts. If you catch yourself thinking negatively, gently guide your thoughts back to a place of understanding and empathy.

Speech is another area where non-violence can be practised. Words have the power to heal or harm, and violent speech can be just as damaging as physical actions. To cultivate non-violence in speech, practice speaking with kindness and consideration. Avoid harsh words, criticism, or gossip. Instead, use your words to uplift and support others. When you communicate with love and respect, you contribute to your inner peace. In terms of actions, non-violence is about consciously choosing to avoid harm to any living being. This includes not only refraining from physical violence but also considering the broader impact of your actions. For example, adopting a vegetarian or plant-based diet is often seen as a practice of non-violence, as it minimises harm to animals. Even in your daily routines, such as driving or interacting with others, practice patience and avoid aggressive behaviours.

Non-violence also means not inflicting harm on yourself. This involves taking care of your body by avoiding harmful substances, getting enough rest, and engaging in practices that promote health and well-being. Treat your body with the same kindness and respect that you would show to others. A life of non-violence fosters inner strength and peace. By choosing non-violence in thought, word, and deed, you purify your existence, creating a space where love, compassion, and positivity can flourish. This practice not only benefits those around you but also deeply enriches your own life, leading to a state of physical and spiritual purity. Through non-violence, you align your actions with the highest ideals of human conduct.

Surround yourself with positive influences:

The people, environments, and ideas that you allow into your life can significantly shape your actions, thoughts, and overall well-being. By consciously choosing to be in the presence of positivity, you cultivate an atmosphere that nurtures your growth and purity.

The company you keep has a profound impact on your life. When you are surrounded by individuals who uplift, inspire, and encourage you, their energy rubs off on you. Positive influences come from people who embody qualities like kindness, honesty, and discipline. These individuals help you stay focused on your goals, offering support and guidance when needed.

On the other hand, negative influences can drain your energy and lead you away from your path. Therefore, it is essential to choose friends, mentors, and colleagues who align with your values and aspirations. The natural world is a powerful influence, reminding you of simplicity and the beauty of life. Spend time in green spaces, listen to the sounds of nature, and let these experiences refresh your mind and body. What you read, watch, and listen to can either uplift you or bring you down. Therefore, choose content that inspires and educates you. Books, podcasts, and media that promote positive thinking, personal growth, and compassion can be incredibly empowering. Avoid content that fosters negativity, violence, or pessimism, as it can subtly affect your mindset.

Surrounding yourself with positive influences is not just about external factors; it also involves cultivating positivity within yourself. Practice gratitude, focus on your strengths, and maintain a hopeful outlook on life. When you embody positivity, you naturally attract similar energy from others. You create an environment that supports your physical and mental well-being. This conscious effort to filter out negativity and embrace uplifting elements helps you stay aligned with your higher purpose.

Avoid addictions:

Addictions, whether to substances like drugs, and alcohol, or habits like excessive screen time and unhealthy eating, can cloud your mind and weaken your body. They trap you in cycles that pull you away from a healthy and balanced life. Breaking free from these chains requires awareness, strength, and commitment, but the rewards are profound. Addictions can be subtle at first, gradually becoming more dominant in your life. What begins as a small indulgence can grow into a powerful habit that is difficult to control. The more you give in to these urges, the more they control you, and the harder it becomes to break free. This is why it is crucial to recognise and address addictive behaviours early on. The journey to overcoming addiction starts with acknowledging the problem and committing to change.

The first step in avoiding addictions is to understand their root cause. Often, addictions arise from an attempt to escape from stress, pain, or dissatisfaction in life. Instead of facing these issues head-on, people might turn to substances or behaviours that offer temporary relief.

However, this relief is fleeting and often comes with damaging consequences. Therefore, it is essential to confront the underlying issues rather than masking them with addictive behaviours.

One powerful way to combat addiction is by cultivating self-discipline and self-control. This involves strengthening your willpower and making conscious choices that align with your goals for purity and well-being. Set clear boundaries for yourself and stick to them. When temptations arise, remind yourself of the long-term benefits of staying on your path.

Another key aspect of avoiding addiction is finding healthy alternatives. Replace destructive habits with positive activities that nourish your body and mind. Exercise, meditation, creative pursuits, and spending time in nature are all excellent ways to fill the void left by addictive behaviours. These activities not only distract you from temptations but also help to rebuild your physical and mental strength.

Avoiding addictions is a continuous journey that requires vigilance and commitment. However, by staying true to your goal of physical purity and adopting positive habits, you can break free from the chains of addiction and lead a healthier, more fulfilling life.

Offer selfless service to others:

It is a powerful way to purify your mind and body. When you engage in acts of kindness without expecting anything in return, you cultivate a spirit of humility, compassion, and inner peace. This selfless service not only benefits others but also deeply transforms you, leading to a purer and more fulfilling life. The practice of selfless service is rooted in the belief that true happiness comes from giving, not receiving. By serving others, you shift your focus from personal desires to the needs of those around you. This shift in perspective helps to dissolve ego and selfishness, which are often the root causes of many negative habits and thoughts. In turn, this purifies your intentions and actions, bringing you closer to a state of physical and mental purity.

One of the key aspects of selfless service is that it must be done without any expectation of recognition or reward. Whether you are helping a friend, volunteering in your community, or simply offering a kind word to someone in need, the act should come from a genuine desire to make a positive impact. This purity of intention is what makes selfless service so transformative. When you serve others without any ulterior motive, you free yourself from the burden of expectations and allow your actions to be guided by love and compassion.

Selfless service also has a profound impact on your physical health. Studies have shown that acts of kindness can reduce stress, lower blood pressure, and even boost your immune system. When you help others, your body releases endorphins, which are natural mood elevators. This not only makes you feel good but also promotes overall well-being. Additionally, selfless service often involves physical activity, whether it's helping someone move, cooking a meal for others, or participating in community clean-ups. This physical engagement keeps your body active and healthy, further contributing to your overall well-being.

Including selfless service in your daily routine is a simple yet powerful way to enhance your physical purity. You don't need to make grand gestures; even small acts of kindness can have a significant impact.

Start by looking for opportunities to help those around you, whether it's your family, friends, or strangers. Over time, this practice will become a natural part of your life, and you will find yourself becoming more compassionate, grounded, and pure. Offering selfless service to others purifies your soul and body. It fosters a deeper connection with the world around you.

Simplify Your Life:

Simplifying your life is a profound step towards achieving physical and mental purity. The modern world is full of complexities and distractions that can easily overwhelm us, making it difficult to focus on what truly matters. By simplifying your life, you create space for clarity, peace, and purposeful living.

At its core, simplifying life is about removing unnecessary clutter, both physical and mental. This process begins with your surroundings. Decluttering your living space helps to create an environment that promotes calmness and order. A clean and organised space reflects a clear mind, making it easier to focus on your goals and maintain discipline. Start by letting go of things that no longer serve you. Whether it's old clothes, gadgets, or even habits, releasing what you don't need helps you feel lighter and more focused. Simplicity also extends to your daily routines. Overcomplicating your schedule with too many commitments can lead to stress and burnout. By prioritising essential tasks and eliminating non-essential ones, you can create a balanced and manageable routine. This doesn't mean doing less, but rather doing what truly matters. Focus on quality over quantity. Engage in activities that nourish your body and mind, such as exercise, meditation, and meaningful work. This approach not only purifies your daily life but also allows you to dedicate more energy to things that bring you joy and fulfilment.

Avoid Criticism:

Criticism, whether directed toward others or oneself, can be corrosive. It breeds negativity, drains energy, and disrupts the peace and harmony that purity seeks to establish. Instead of engaging in criticism, adopting a mindset of understanding, compassion, and acceptance brings us closer to living a pure and fulfilling life.

Criticism often stems from internal dissatisfaction or the need to feel superior. When we criticise others, we are essentially focusing on their flaws rather than their strengths. This habit not only impacts those around us but also affects our mental and physical well-being. Constant negativity can lead to stress, tension, and even physical ailments. On the other hand, avoiding criticism helps maintain a positive mindset, which is essential for a healthy life.

One effective way to avoid criticism is by practising empathy. Putting yourself in someone else's shoes allows you to see the world from their perspective. This broader viewpoint helps in understanding their actions and reduces the tendency to judge. When we approach situations with empathy, we are more likely to respond with kindness and support rather than criticism. This approach not only fosters better relationships but also purifies our interactions with others, creating a more harmonious environment. Another important step is self-awareness. Often, the criticism we direct at others is a reflection of our own insecurities or unmet expectations. Avoiding self-criticism is equally important. Negative self-talk can be just as damaging as criticising others. It can lead to low self-esteem, and anxiety, and hinder personal growth. The journey towards purity is enhanced when you choose to uplift rather than criticise.

Avoid Toxic Relationships:

Toxic relationships, whether with friends, family, or colleagues, can be detrimental to your well-being and disrupt your inner peace. These relationships often drain your energy, foster negativity, and create emotional turmoil, making it difficult to maintain a balanced and healthy life. A toxic relationship is characterised by consistent negativity, manipulation, control, and lack of respect. Being involved in such relationships can lead to stress, anxiety, and a decrease in self-esteem. Over time, the impact of toxic relationships can also manifest physically, affecting your overall health and vitality. By avoiding such relationships, you safeguard your mental and physical health, allowing yourself to thrive in a positive and supportive environment.

To avoid toxic relationships, it is important first to recognise the signs. Toxic relationships often involve persistent negativity, disrespect, and a lack of genuine support. You may feel constantly criticised, manipulated, or belittled. Identifying these patterns early on allows you to take steps to distance yourself from individuals who do not contribute positively to your life. It is important to enforce these boundaries consistently to maintain your emotional well-being. Seek relationships that uplift you, encourage your growth, and bring out the best in you. Positive relationships contribute to a healthy and joyful life, enhancing your overall sense of well-being. Invest in connections that are based on mutual respect, understanding, and support.

Summary:

In this chapter, we focused on achieving physical purity through a series of impactful practices. We began with practising cleanliness and wearing clean clothes, emphasising that hygiene reflects and contributes to inner purity. Eating good food and detoxification were highlighted as essential for maintaining a healthy body. We also discussed maintaining a clean living space to create a harmonious environment. Eliminating negative habits and avoiding addictions help in fostering mental and physical health. By practising non-violence and offering selfless service, we promote a positive, compassionate lifestyle. Surrounding yourself with positive influences and avoiding toxic relationships safeguard your well-being while simplifying your life and avoiding criticism reduce stress and enhance personal growth. These practices collectively contribute to a purer, more balanced life, setting the foundation for better well-being.

Chapter 3 – Physical Strength

Source: 75suryanamaskar.com

> *"The world is the great gymnasium where we come to make ourselves strong."*
>
> *–Swami Vivekananda*

Life itself provides endless opportunities for physical growth and resilience. Just as a gymnasium offers challenges to build strength, the world presents us with daily trials that can be used to enhance our physical fitness. Engaging in outdoor activities, practising sports, or simply embracing physical challenges helps us grow stronger, both in body and mind. By treating the world as our gym, we can use every experience (be it strenuous or mundane) to push our limits and achieve greater physical health and endurance.

Building Stamina:

It is a journey that requires consistency, determination, and a systematic approach. Stamina is not just about enduring physical activities for long periods but also about sustaining energy and vitality throughout daily life. The process of building stamina involves cultivating both physical and mental resilience.

One of the key practices in building stamina is regular exercise. Engaging in activities like

running, swimming, or cycling can help improve cardiovascular health, which is crucial for endurance. Start with manageable distances or times, and gradually increase the intensity and duration of your workouts. This gradual approach prevents burnout and injury while allowing the body to adapt to increased demands. Consistency is important; make exercise a regular part of your routine rather than an occasional effort.

Another important practice is proper breathing. Learning to control your breath during physical activity can greatly enhance stamina. Deep, rhythmic breathing helps oxygenate your muscles, allowing you to sustain physical exertion for longer periods. Practices like pranayama (breath control exercises) can be beneficial for developing this skill. By focusing on your breath, you also train your mind to stay calm and focused during challenging physical tasks.

Nutrition plays a significant role in building stamina. Eating a balanced diet that includes complex carbohydrates, proteins, and healthy fats provides the fuel your body needs for sustained energy. Hydration is equally important; drinking enough water before, during, and after exercise ensures that your body functions optimally. Avoid heavy, greasy foods that can weigh you down and slow your progress. Rest and recovery are often overlooked aspects of building stamina, but they are just as important as exercise. Giving your body time to recover after strenuous activity helps prevent fatigue and injury. Adequate sleep is crucial; aim for at least seven to eight hours of restful sleep each night to allow your body to repair and rejuvenate.

Mentally, building stamina requires a positive mindset. Cultivate patience and perseverance, understanding that progress may be slow but steady. Visualise your goals and stay motivated by reminding yourself of the benefits of increased stamina, whether it's improved health, better performance in sports, or simply feeling more energetic in daily life.

Strengthening Muscles:

Strengthening muscles requires consistent effort, focus, and a dedicated approach. Strong muscles not only enhance physical performance but also contribute to overall health, stability, and resilience in daily life. To effectively strengthen your muscles, it's essential to adopt a balanced routine that incorporates both physical exercises and mindful practices.

Exercises like weightlifting, push-ups, squats, and lunges are excellent for building muscle mass and strength. Start with lighter weights or bodyweight exercises, focusing on proper form to avoid injury. Gradually increase the resistance or weight as your muscles adapt and grow stronger. Consistency is crucial. Regular workouts, whether it's three to four times a week, help build and maintain muscle strength over time.

Including exercises that improve flexibility and balance is also important. Stretching exercises like yoga can enhance muscle elasticity and prevent stiffness, which is essential for preventing injuries and maintaining overall muscle health. Flexibility helps in performing exercises more effectively and ensures that muscles work efficiently. Another vital component of muscle strengthening is proper nutrition. Muscles need adequate protein to repair and grow after workouts. Include a variety of protein-rich foods in your diet, such as beans and nuts. Don't forget to balance your diet with carbohydrates and healthy fats, which provide the energy needed for intense workouts and muscle recovery. Hydration is equally important to keep your muscles functioning optimally. Embrace challenges as opportunities to grow stronger, both physically and mentally.

Endurance Training:

Endurance training involves training your body to perform sustained physical activities over extended periods without fatigue. The key to effective endurance training is consistency, gradual progression, and a systematic approach that strengthens both the body and the mind.

One of the best practices for endurance training is to start with cardiovascular exercises that elevate your heart rate and keep it elevated for a prolonged period. Activities like running, cycling, swimming, and brisk walking are excellent for this purpose. Start with a manageable pace and duration (perhaps 20 to 30 minutes a few times a week) and gradually increase the intensity and length of your workouts as your endurance improves. The goal is to push your limits in a controlled manner, allowing your body to adapt and grow stronger over time.

Incorporating interval training is another effective strategy for building endurance. This involves alternating between periods of high-intensity exercise and low-intensity recovery. For example, if you're running, you might sprint for 30 seconds and then walk for 60 seconds before repeating the cycle. Interval training challenges your cardiovascular system and helps improve both your speed and endurance.

While it may seem counterintuitive, building muscle strength supports your endurance efforts. Exercises like squats, lunges, push-ups, and planks help strengthen the muscles that support your cardiovascular activities. Aim to include strength training exercises in your routine two to three times a week, focusing on all major muscle groups.

Your body needs the right fuel to sustain long periods of activity. A balanced diet rich in complex carbohydrates, lean proteins, and healthy fats provides the energy required for endurance workouts. Carbohydrates are particularly important because they are the body's primary source of energy during prolonged exercise. Include whole grains, fruits, vegetables, and legumes in your meals to keep your energy levels steady. Additionally, staying hydrated is essential, as even mild dehydration can impair endurance performance. Drink water before, during, and after your workouts to maintain optimal hydration levels.

Cultivating a strong mindset is essential to push through these barriers. Set clear goals for your training and break them down into smaller milestones that you can celebrate along the way. Visualisation techniques can also be powerful (imagine yourself succeeding and reaching your endurance goals). This mental imagery can motivate you to keep going even when the physical effort becomes tough.

Physical Flexibility:

Physical flexibility not only enhances physical performance but also reduces the risk of injury, improves posture, and promotes better circulation. Achieving and maintaining flexibility requires a balanced approach, combining regular practice, mindfulness, and patience.

One of the best practices to enhance flexibility is through consistent stretching exercises. Stretching should be a regular part of your daily routine, just like any other form of exercise. Start your day with gentle stretches to loosen up your muscles and prepare your body for the activities ahead. Focus on dynamic stretching in the morning, which involves controlled movements that gently take your joints and muscles through their full range of motion. Examples include leg swings, arm circles, and gentle spinal twists. After physical activity, static stretching is beneficial. This involves holding a stretch for 20 to 30 seconds, allowing your muscles to relax and lengthen. Target major muscle groups such as your hamstrings, quadriceps, calves, shoulders, and back. By focusing on these areas, you can enhance flexibility in your entire body.

Another effective practice to improve flexibility is yoga. Yoga combines stretching, strength, and mindfulness, making it a better approach to flexibility training. Regular yoga practice not only stretches the muscles but also promotes better alignment, breathing, and mental focus. Poses like the downward dog, forward fold, and cobra are excellent for lengthening muscles and improving joint mobility. Incorporating yoga into your routine can also help relieve tension and reduce stress, further aiding in flexibility.

Maintaining a healthy lifestyle is essential for flexibility. Staying hydrated is key because dehydrated muscles can become stiff and less pliable, making it harder to achieve and maintain flexibility. Foods high in antioxidants, like fruits and vegetables, can reduce inflammation and promote muscle repair, allowing your body to stretch more effectively. Omega-3 fatty acids found in fish, nuts, and seeds can also reduce muscle stiffness and improve joint health.

While improving flexibility, approach flexibility training with patience and awareness. Stretch to the point of mild discomfort, but never to the point of pain. Over time, your muscles will adapt, and your flexibility will gradually increase. Like any other aspect of physical fitness, flexibility improves with regular practice. Make stretching and mobility exercises a part of your daily routine, even on rest days. Over time, you'll notice increased ease of movement, reduced stiffness, and improved overall performance in your physical activities.

Flexibility is not just a physical attribute but also a reflection of your mental state. Approaching your practice with openness, patience, and perseverance will yield better results. Celebrate small improvements, and remember that flexibility is a journey, not a destination. Stay committed to the practice, listen to your body, and approach your flexibility training with a positive mindset. Over time, you'll find yourself moving with greater ease and grace, ready to tackle any physical challenge.

Overcoming Physical Weakness:

Physical weakness can manifest in different ways, whether it's a lack of energy, muscle weakness, or difficulty in performing daily tasks. However, by focusing on key practices and maintaining a disciplined lifestyle, one can gradually overcome these challenges and build a strong foundation for physical strength.

The first step in overcoming physical weakness is understanding its root cause. Self-awareness is crucial; pay attention to your body and identify the areas where you feel weak or struggle. Is it a lack of stamina, muscle strength, or energy levels? Knowing where your weaknesses lie allows you to target those specific areas with focused efforts.

Incorporate a mix of cardiovascular exercises, strength training, and flexibility exercises. Cardiovascular exercises like walking, cycling, or swimming can improve your heart health and increase your endurance. Strength training exercises, such as bodyweight exercises, resistance bands, or weightlifting, help build muscle mass and combat muscle weakness. When working on overcoming physical weakness, it's essential to progress gradually. Avoid the temptation to push yourself too hard too soon, as this can lead to injury and setbacks. Start with low-impact exercises and gradually increase the intensity as your body becomes stronger. Patience is key; give your body time to adapt and build strength over time.

Overcoming physical weakness isn't just a physical challenge; it's also a mental one. Cultivate a mindset of resilience and determination. Understand that setbacks are a natural part of the journey and that progress may be slow. Instead of becoming discouraged, use each setback as a learning experience and stay committed to your goals. Mental resilience will help you push through difficult times and stay on track. If your physical weakness is persistent or if you're unsure about how to address it, seeking professional guidance can be invaluable. Consult a fitness trainer, physical therapist, or healthcare professional who can assess your condition and provide personalised advice. They can help you create a tailored exercise and nutrition plan that addresses your specific needs and ensures that you're progressing safely and effectively.

Surround yourself with a supportive community. Share your goals with them, celebrate your progress, and lean on them during tough times. A strong support system can provide the motivation and accountability you need to keep moving forward.

Balancing Strength and Agility:

Strength provides the power to perform tasks effectively, while agility allows for quick and efficient movement. When combined, they enhance overall performance, enabling the body to function at its best in both everyday activities and more demanding physical challenges. Achieving a balance between these two aspects requires thoughtful planning, discipline, and a focus on key practices that promote both power and fluidity.

Strength and agility are often seen as separate components of fitness, but they are deeply interconnected. Strength gives you the foundation to lift, push, and endure physical stress, while agility allows you to move with speed, change direction smoothly, and react swiftly to external stimuli. When balanced, these two elements ensure that your body is not only powerful but also adaptable and responsive. Functional training is a key practice in balancing strength and agility. This type of exercise focuses on movements that mimic everyday activities, engaging multiple muscle groups and promoting coordination. By incorporating functional training into your routine, you develop the ability to move efficiently in different directions while maintaining control and stability.

A well-rounded fitness routine should include both strength-building exercises and agility drills. For strength, incorporate exercises such as weightlifting, bodyweight exercises, or resistance band workouts. These exercises target major muscle groups, building the power needed for various tasks. To enhance agility, include drills that improve speed, coordination, and reaction time. Activities like ladder drills, cone drills, and plyometric exercises (e.g., jump squats or box jumps) train your body to move quickly and accurately. A strong core is crucial for both strength and agility. The core muscles stabilise the body, allowing for smooth transitions between movements and supporting powerful actions. Strengthen your core through exercises like planks, Russian twists, and leg raises. These exercises not only enhance your overall strength but also improve your balance and control, making you more agile and less prone to injury.

Mindful movement can help you balance strength and agility by ensuring that each movement is purposeful and controlled. Techniques such as tai chi or mindful yoga encourage you to focus on your breath and body alignment, promoting smooth, coordinated movements. This awareness enhances both strength and agility, as you learn to engage the right muscles at the right time. Interval training, which alternates between high-intensity exercises and periods of rest or lower intensity, is an effective way to build both strength and agility. For example, you can combine short bursts of sprinting with strength exercises like push-ups or squats. This method trains your body to handle different levels of intensity and improves both power and speed. Interval training is also time-efficient, making it easier to fit into a busy schedule. Techniques like foam rolling, massages, and adequate sleep can aid in recovery, ensuring that your muscles are ready for the next challenge.

Nature Walks:

Nature walks offer a simple yet powerful way to enhance physical strength while connecting with the natural world. Walking through diverse terrains, such as forests, hills, or along riversides, engages various muscle groups and promotes overall physical fitness. But nature walks go beyond just building strength; they also improve mental well-being, reduce stress, and offer a break from the hustle and bustle of everyday life.

Nature walks are an excellent way to build physical strength because they engage multiple muscle groups simultaneously. Walking on uneven terrain, climbing hills, and navigating through rocky paths require the use of leg muscles, core muscles, and even the upper body for balance. Over time, this consistent engagement strengthens muscles and improves endurance, making your body stronger and more resilient. Walking, especially in nature, is a great cardiovascular exercise. It increases heart rate, improves circulation, and enhances lung capacity. Regular nature walks can help lower blood pressure, reduce the risk of heart disease, and boost overall cardiovascular health. The combination of fresh air and physical activity creates a perfect environment for a healthy heart. Nature walks often involve navigating through uneven terrain, and stepping over roots, rocks, and streams. These movements require flexibility and balance, which are essential components of physical strength. By regularly walking in nature, you naturally improve your balance and flexibility, making your body more adaptable and less prone to injury.

Spending time in nature has a profound impact on mental health. The peaceful environment, coupled with physical activity, reduces stress, anxiety, and depression. It provides an opportunity to disconnect from technology and the stresses of daily life, allowing your mind to relax and rejuvenate. This mental clarity and calmness contribute to overall well-being, making you feel more energised and motivated. Nature walks offer a unique opportunity to connect with the environment around you. Observing the beauty of trees, flowers, wildlife, and the changing seasons fosters a sense of appreciation and gratitude. This connection to nature not only nurtures the soul but also encourages a healthier lifestyle. It reminds you of the importance of taking care of your body, just as you take care of the earth. To fully reap the benefits of nature walks, make them a regular part of your routine. Whether it's a daily walk in the park, a weekend hike, or a visit to a nature reserve. The more you walk, the stronger and more energised you will feel.

The Power of Posture:

Posture plays a crucial role in your physical strength and overall well-being. It's more than just standing or sitting up straight; posture affects how you move, breathe, and even think. Proper posture aligns your body, reduces strain on muscles and joints, and promotes better physical performance. Good posture ensures that your body is properly aligned. When you stand, sit, or move with correct alignment, your bones, muscles, and joints work together efficiently. This alignment reduces unnecessary strain on your muscles and ligaments, preventing fatigue and injury. Over time, proper posture strengthens your core, back, and other muscle groups, making you physically stronger and more resilient.

Posture directly influences your breathing. When you slouch or hunch over, your chest compresses, and your lungs have less room to expand. This limits your oxygen intake, which can lead to fatigue and decreased energy levels. On the other hand, maintaining good posture opens up your chest and allows for deeper, more efficient breathing. Better breathing improves your endurance, concentration, and overall vitality.

Your posture reflects your state of mind. Standing tall with your shoulders back and head held high projects confidence and self-assurance. This not only affects how others perceive you but also influences how you feel about yourself. Good posture encourages positive thinking, boosts self-esteem, and can even improve your mood. Whether you're lifting weights, practising yoga, or simply going about your daily activities, good posture enhances your physical performance. It provides a stable foundation for movement, allowing you to use your muscles more effectively. With proper posture, you can lift heavier weights, move more efficiently and reduce the risk of injury. This improved physical performance contributes to greater overall strength and fitness.

Poor posture is a common cause of back, neck, and shoulder pain. Slouching or misaligning your body places extra pressure on your spine and muscles, leading to discomfort and long-term issues. By practising good posture, you can alleviate and prevent pain, keeping your body in optimal condition. This not only makes you physically stronger but also allows you to stay active and engaged in life.

Restorative Practices:

Whether it's the physical demands of work, exercise, or the mental stress from daily life, it's easy to become worn out and depleted. That's where restorative practices come into play. These are techniques and habits designed to help you recover, rejuvenate, and maintain balance in your life. By incorporating restorative practices, you can not only recover from physical and mental exhaustion but also build resilience for future challenges.

Restorative practices emphasise the importance of rest and recovery as essential components of physical and mental strength. Just as muscles need time to repair and grow after a workout, your entire body requires periods of rest to function optimally. Without adequate rest, you risk burnout, injuries, and reduced performance. Restorative practices help replenish your energy, repair tissues, and restore mental clarity.

Yoga and stretching are key restorative practices that promote flexibility, reduce tension, and calm the mind. Gentle yoga poses, such as child's pose, legs-up-the-wall, and savasana, help relax your muscles and release stress. Stretching after workouts or at the end of the day can prevent stiffness, enhance circulation, and improve your overall range of motion.

Breathing exercises are simple yet powerful restorative practices that help reduce stress and improve lung capacity. Techniques such as deep diaphragmatic breathing, alternate nostril breathing, and box breathing can calm your nervous system and promote relaxation. These exercises are particularly helpful during moments of high stress or anxiety, allowing you to regain control and focus. Regular practice can improve your breathing efficiency and support your overall health. Active recovery involves engaging in low-intensity activities that promote blood flow and muscle repair without putting additional strain on your body. This can include walking, swimming, or light cycling. Active recovery helps flush out lactic acid, reduce muscle soreness, and keep your body limber. It's an excellent way to stay active while giving your body the time it needs to heal.

Massage and physical therapy are effective restorative practices that can help alleviate muscle tension, improve circulation, and enhance recovery. Regular massages can prevent injuries, reduce pain, and promote relaxation. Physical therapy, on the other hand, is particularly useful for recovering from injuries and improving mobility. Both practices contribute to your overall physical well-being and help you maintain strength and flexibility. Restorative practices aren't just about physical recovery; emotional restoration is equally important. Engaging in activities that bring you joy, spending time with loved ones, or pursuing hobbies can help recharge your emotional energy. Journaling, therapy, or talking to a friend can also be valuable in processing emotions and reducing stress. Emotional well-being is a key component of overall health and emotional restoration.

Resilience Training:

Resilience is the ability to bounce back from challenges, setbacks, and adversities. It's the inner strength that helps you face difficulties with courage, adapt to change, and keep moving forward despite the obstacles. Resilience training involves cultivating this mental and emotional toughness so you can navigate life's ups and downs with grace and determination. It's not about avoiding problems but learning how to handle them effectively.

Resilience is built through experience, particularly by facing challenges head-on. Rather than avoiding difficult situations, embrace them as opportunities for growth. Every challenge you overcome adds to your resilience, making you better equipped to handle future obstacles. It's important to see challenges not as threats but as chances to strengthen your skills and character. Physical and mental well-being are crucial components of resilience. When you take care of your body through proper nutrition, exercise, and sleep, you're better equipped to handle stress. Similarly, practices like mindfulness, meditation, and relaxation techniques help keep your mind clear and focused. Self-care isn't a luxury; it's a necessity for maintaining the strength to face life's challenges. Resilience training also involves cultivating emotional awareness. Being in tune with your emotions helps you understand how challenges are affecting you, which in turn enables you to respond effectively. Instead of suppressing feelings like frustration or sadness, acknowledge them and explore ways to manage them. Emotional intelligence (knowing how to identify, understand, and regulate emotions) strengthens your resilience by helping you stay balanced and composed under pressure.

When confronted with a difficult situation, break it down into manageable parts and explore different solutions. Flexibility and creativity in problem-solving allow you to adapt to changing circumstances and find ways around obstacles. Over time, honing these skills builds your confidence and resilience, as you become more capable of handling whatever comes your way. Setbacks and failures are inevitable, but they don't have to define you. Resilience involves viewing setbacks as learning experiences rather than permanent defeats. Reflect on what went wrong, what you can learn from the situation, and how you can improve moving forward. Each setback is an opportunity to grow and become more resilient.

Setting realistic, achievable goals is another key aspect of resilience training. When your goals are clear and within reach, you're less likely to feel overwhelmed by challenges. Break larger goals into smaller, manageable steps and celebrate your progress along the way. Achieving these milestones reinforces your resilience by showing you that progress is possible even in the face of difficulties.

Gratitude is a powerful tool for building resilience. By focusing on what you have rather than what you lack, you shift your perspective from scarcity to abundance. Adaptability is a key trait of resilient individuals. Stay open to change, be willing to modify your plans if necessary, and remain flexible in your approach. Mental toughness involves developing the mental grit to persevere through difficult situations. It's about pushing through discomfort, maintaining focus, and staying committed to your goals even when the going gets tough.

Having a sense of purpose gives you direction and motivation, especially during tough times. When you're connected to a higher purpose (whether it's a personal mission, a passion, or a belief system), you're more likely to stay resilient in the face of adversity. Purpose provides meaning to your efforts and helps you stay committed, even when challenges arise.

Strengthening the Immune System:

A strong immune system is essential for maintaining good health and protecting the body from infections, illnesses, and diseases. Strengthening the immune system includes proper nutrition, regular exercise, adequate sleep, stress management, and adopting healthy lifestyle habits. By focusing on these areas, you can build a resilient immune system that can effectively ward off illnesses and keep you feeling your best.

Eating a variety of nutrient-rich foods provides your body with the essential vitamins, minerals, and antioxidants it needs to function optimally. Include plenty of fruits and vegetables, which are high in vitamins C and E, as well as beta-carotene and zinc. These nutrients help support immune function by protecting cells from damage and promoting the production of white blood cells, which are key players in fighting infections. Include whole grains, lean proteins, and healthy fats in your diet as well. Foods like garlic, ginger, and turmeric have natural anti-inflammatory and immune-boosting properties. Probiotics, found in yoghurt and fermented foods like sauerkraut and kimchi, support gut health, which is closely linked to immune function. A healthy gut microbiome plays a crucial role in defending the body against harmful pathogens.

Physical activity is another important factor in strengthening the immune system. Exercise also reduces inflammation and supports the body's natural detoxification processes. Aim for at least 30 minutes of moderate exercise most days of the week. Activities like walking, jogging, cycling, or swimming can help keep your immune system in top shape. However, it's important to strike a balance; over-exercising or pushing your body too hard can weaken the immune system, so moderation is key. Lack of sleep can reduce the production of these protective proteins, making you more susceptible to infections. Aim for 7-9 hours of quality sleep each night.

Chronic stress can weaken the immune system by elevating cortisol levels, which suppresses immune function. Managing stress is therefore essential for maintaining a strong immune system.

Incorporate relaxation techniques such as deep breathing, meditation, or yoga into your daily routine to help manage stress levels. Engaging in activities you enjoy, spending time with loved ones, and practising mindfulness can all contribute to a more balanced and resilient immune system. Taking regular breaks and ensuring you have time to unwind can also reduce the impact of stress on your health.

Certain habits, such as smoking and excessive alcohol consumption, can weaken the immune system and increase the risk of infections. Smoking damages the lungs and impairs the immune response, while excessive alcohol intake can disrupt the balance of immune cells in the body. Reducing or eliminating these habits can significantly improve your immune health. Regular health check-ups and screenings are essential for monitoring your immune health and overall well-being. These check-ups can help detect any potential issues early on and allow you to take preventive measures. Staying on top of vaccinations is also important, as vaccines can help prevent infections and strengthen your immune response.

Good hygiene practices are fundamental to protecting the immune system from infections. Washing your hands regularly, especially before eating and after being in public places, can prevent the spread of harmful germs. Spending time outdoors in fresh air and sunlight can also boost your immune system. Sunlight helps the body produce vitamin D, which plays a crucial role in immune function. Vitamin D helps regulate the immune response and has been shown to reduce the risk of respiratory infections. Try to get at least 15-30 minutes of sun exposure each day, but be mindful of protecting your skin from overexposure. A positive mindset and emotional well-being are closely linked to immune health. Studies have shown that people with a positive outlook on life tend to have stronger immune systems and are better able to fight off infections.

Mastering Balance:

Balance is not just about standing on one leg or avoiding a fall; it involves coordinating the body, mind, and senses to achieve stability and harmony in movement and posture. Mastering balance is crucial for daily activities, athletic performance, and injury prevention. Developing balance also enhances mental focus and body awareness, leading to a more confident and composed approach to life.

It involves a complex interaction between the brain, muscles, joints, and sensory systems like vision and the inner ear. Good balance allows us to move efficiently, maintain proper posture, and react quickly to changes in our environment. As we age, balance can decline, making it even more important to actively work on maintaining and improving it. A strong core is the foundation of good balance. The core muscles, including the abdominals, back, and pelvis, support the spine and provide stability during movement. Exercises like planks, bridges, and leg lifts can help build core strength and improve overall balance.

Start with simple exercises, such as standing on one leg for a few seconds, and gradually increase the difficulty by closing your eyes or performing the exercise on an unstable surface like a balance board. Balance is not just physical; it also involves mental focus and awareness. The mind-body connection is crucial in mastering balance. Being mindful of your body's position and movement helps you make adjustments and maintain stability. Functional balance training focuses on improving balance in everyday activities, such as walking, climbing stairs, or reaching for objects. Exercises like lunges, squats, and step-ups mimic these movements and help improve balance in real-life situations. Incorporating functional training into your routine ensures that your balance skills are transferable to daily activities.

The visual and vestibular systems play a critical role in maintaining balance. Your eyes provide information about your surroundings, while the vestibular system in the inner ear helps you sense changes in head position and movement. To challenge and improve these systems, practice balance exercises with your eyes closed or in low-light conditions. This forces your body to rely more on other senses, like proprioception (the sense of body position), to maintain balance. Progress may be slow at first, but with consistent practice, you will see improvement. Celebrate small victories along the way, and don't be discouraged by setbacks. Remember that balance is a skill that can be developed over time with dedication and effort.

Physical Courage:

Physical courage is the ability to confront fear, pain, danger, or adversity in the physical realm. It's not just about bravery in the face of danger; it also involves the resilience to endure hardships, the willpower to push through physical limits, and the determination to stand firm even when the body feels like giving up. Physical courage is a crucial trait for anyone aiming to achieve strength, resilience, and mastery over their own body.

One of the most significant aspects of physical courage is the willingness to face challenges head-on, despite fear or discomfort. Whether it's engaging in a demanding workout, participating in a strenuous sport, or even standing up for yourself in a physical confrontation, physical courage drives you to push through barriers. It involves recognising your fears but not allowing them to control your actions. Physical courage goes hand in hand with resilience. It's the ability to recover quickly from injuries, setbacks, or failures. Resilience is essential when you're pursuing any physical goal because setbacks are inevitable. Whether it's an injury during training or a loss in competition, physical courage gives you the strength to bounce back, recover, and continue your pursuit.

Pain is a natural part of any physical endeavour, whether it's from intense exercise, injury, or the physical discomfort of pushing your body beyond its limits. Physical courage is what helps you endure pain and keep going. It's important, however, to distinguish between productive pain, which can lead to growth and improvement, and harmful pain, which could signal injury. The courage lies in knowing when to push through and when to stop.

Physical courage is about committing to continuous growth and improvement, no matter how difficult the journey may be. This requires stepping out of your comfort zone and facing physical challenges that test your limits. Whether it's lifting heavier weights, running longer distances, or mastering a new skill, the courage to keep striving for improvement is what leads to growth. Discipline is a key factor in cultivating physical courage. It's the discipline that keeps you consistent in your training, even when you're tired or unmotivated. It's the discipline that makes you get up early to exercise, follow a healthy diet, and stick to your goals. Physical courage often involves overcoming inner battles against laziness, procrastination, or fear, and discipline is the tool that helps you win those battles.

Physical courage also involves setting an example for others. When you demonstrate courage in your physical endeavours, you inspire those around you to do the same. Whether it's through your determination to overcome obstacles or your ability to stay calm and composed under pressure, your courage can motivate others to push through their own challenges. Fear is a natural emotion, especially when facing physical challenges that involve risk. Physical courage doesn't mean being fearless; it means acting despite your fears. Whether it's the fear of injury, failure, or the unknown, courage is what propels you forward. By confronting and embracing fear, you not only become stronger physically but mentally as well.

Physical courage also extends to self-protection and defending others when necessary. It involves the willingness to take action when you or someone else is in danger. This could mean standing up to a threat, protecting others, or even learning self-defence techniques to ensure your safety. Physical courage in this context is about being prepared to act when needed. It's the realisation that challenges and obstacles are part of the process, and each one is an opportunity to grow stronger. By accepting the difficulties that come with physical pursuits, you develop a deeper sense of courage that transcends the physical and permeates all aspects of your life.

Listening to Your Body:

Listening to your body is an essential practice in maintaining physical health, preventing injury, and achieving long-term well-being. Often, we push ourselves too hard in the pursuit of fitness goals or ignore the signals our bodies send us, which can lead to burnout, fatigue, or even serious injury. The wisdom of listening to your body teaches us the importance of being in tune with ourselves, recognising our limits, and responding appropriately to the cues our body provides. Your body constantly communicates with you, offering signals that reflect its current state. These signals include feelings of fatigue, pain, hunger, thirst, and even mood changes. By paying attention to these signals, you can make informed decisions about your physical activities, rest, and nutrition.

Physical fitness is not just about pushing yourself to the limit; it's also about knowing when to rest. Recovery is a crucial aspect of any fitness regimen, allowing your muscles to heal and grow stronger. Ignoring the need for rest can lead to overtraining, which can weaken your immune system, increase the risk of injury, and decrease performance. Listening to your body ensures that you strike a balance between effort and recovery, optimising your results.

It's important to distinguish between discomfort, which is a natural part of physical exertion, and pain, which can indicate an injury or overexertion. Discomfort during exercise, such as muscle soreness, is often a sign that you're challenging your body and making progress. However, sharp or persistent pain is your body's way of telling you that something is wrong. Pushing through pain can worsen injuries and hinder your progress. By listening to your body, you can avoid these setbacks and take steps to address issues before they escalate. Your body's needs and abilities can change over time due to factors such as age, lifestyle, and overall health. Being attuned to these changes allows you to adapt your physical activities accordingly. For instance, as you age, you might need to incorporate more flexibility exercises, low-impact activities, or longer recovery periods. Listening to your body helps you make these adjustments, ensuring that your fitness routine remains sustainable and effective.

Listening to your body also involves recognising its nutritional needs. Hunger and thirst are clear signals that your body needs fuel and hydration. Ignoring these signals can lead to energy depletion, decreased performance, and even health issues. It's important to nourish your body with the right foods and fluids, especially before and after physical activity, to maintain optimal performance and recovery. Your mental and emotional state is closely linked to your physical well-being. Stress, anxiety, and emotional exhaustion can manifest physically, leading to fatigue, tension, or a lack of motivation. Listening to your body means being aware of these emotional and mental cues as well.

In a world where fitness goals and achievements are often shared on social media, it's easy to fall into the trap of comparing yourself to others. However, everyone's body is unique, and what works for someone else may not work for you. Listening to your body means respecting your own pace, limitations, and progress, rather than trying to match someone else's standards. This approach fosters a healthier and more sustainable relationship with your body.

Intuition plays a key role in listening to your body. Sometimes, you may feel an inexplicable urge to rest, stretch, or change your routine, even if you can't pinpoint a specific reason. Trusting your intuition is part of being in tune with your body's needs. This intuitive connection strengthens, allowing you to make better decisions for your physical health.

Streamlining Physical Exercise:

Streamlining physical exercise is about optimising your routine, focusing on efficiency, and ensuring that every movement counts. This method not only saves time but also keeps you motivated and consistent in your fitness journey. One of the most effective ways to streamline your workouts is by focusing on core exercises that target multiple muscle groups simultaneously. These compound exercises, such as squats, deadlifts, push-ups, and pull-ups, provide maximum benefits in a shorter time frame. By engaging several muscles at once, you improve strength, balance, and endurance without needing to spend hours at the gym.

Having clear fitness goals is essential for streamlining your exercise routine. Whether you want to build muscle, lose weight, improve cardiovascular health, or increase flexibility, knowing your goals helps you tailor your workouts to meet your specific needs. This focus prevents you from wasting time on exercises that don't align with your objectives. Create a plan that includes the most effective exercises for achieving your goals, and stick to it.

High-Intensity Interval Training (HIIT) is an excellent way to maximise your workout efficiency. This training method alternates between short bursts of intense exercise and periods of rest or lower-intensity exercise. HIIT sessions typically last between 20 to 30 minutes but can deliver the same, if not better, results than longer workouts. It's particularly effective for burning fat, boosting metabolism, and improving cardiovascular health. One of the key aspects of streamlining exercise is managing your time effectively. Dedicate specific time slots for your workouts and stick to them. Morning workouts, for example, can energise you for the day ahead and ensure that exercise doesn't get pushed aside by other responsibilities. Keep your workouts short but intense, focusing on quality over quantity. If you only have 20-30 minutes a day, make those minutes count with focused, goal-oriented exercises.

Functional movements mimic everyday activities and enhance your ability to perform daily tasks. By incorporating exercises like lunges, planks, and kettlebell swings, you not only streamline your workouts but also improve your overall mobility and strength in real-life situations. This approach ensures that your exercise routine is practical and directly beneficial to your daily life. Instead of separating strength training and cardio into different sessions, combine them for a more efficient workout. Circuit training, for example, allows you to alternate between strength exercises and cardio exercises, keeping your heart rate up while also building muscle. This method reduces the time spent in the gym while delivering comprehensive fitness benefits.

Bodyweight exercises, such as push-ups, squats, and burpees, are excellent for streamlining your workouts. They require no equipment, can be done anywhere, and provide a full-body workout. Bodyweight exercises can be easily modified to increase or decrease intensity, making them suitable for all fitness levels. Plus, they allow you to work out whenever and wherever you have time, eliminating the need for a gym visit. To make the most of your workout time, plan your sessions in advance. Know exactly which exercises you'll do, how many sets and reps, and the duration of your workout before you start. This eliminates downtime spent deciding what to do next and keeps your workout focused and efficient. Having a plan also makes it easier to track your progress over time. Streamlining your exercise doesn't mean cutting out the fun. Include activities you love, whether it's dancing, swimming, hiking, or playing a sport. When you enjoy your workouts, you're more likely to stick with them, making consistency easier to achieve.

Physical Grace:

Physical grace is the harmonious blend of strength, control, and awareness that allows one to move effortlessly through space. Achieving physical grace is not just about external appearance; it's a reflection of inner balance, mindfulness, and confidence.

To develop physical grace, the first step is to become more aware of your movements. This involves paying attention to how you walk, sit, stand, and perform daily activities. Mindful movement is key. When you're aware of your body, you can make adjustments to move with more fluidity and precision. Whether you're walking down the street or performing a complex exercise, focus on each movement and strive for smooth transitions. These practices teach you to move with intention, aligning your body and creating a sense of flow in your movements.

By synchronising your breath with your movements, you create a natural rhythm that enhances your flow and grace. In activities like yoga or dance, focusing on your breath can help you move with more control and ease. Deep, steady breathing calms the mind and allows your body to move in harmony with itself. Confidence in your movements makes them appear more fluid and purposeful. Practice self-assurance in your posture and the way you carry yourself. Being fully present in the moment, whether you're exercising, dancing, or simply walking, helps you move with more grace. When you're connected to your body and mind, your movements become a natural expression of who you are.

You don't need to be a dancer or athlete to cultivate physical grace. It can be integrated into everyday activities. Simple acts like rising from a chair, reaching for an object, or greeting someone can be done with grace when you approach them with mindfulness and intention. Observe dancers, athletes, or even people in your daily life who move with elegance. Notice their posture, the fluidity of their movements, and how they carry themselves. By observing and emulating their grace, you can incorporate these qualities into your movements. With time, the deliberate practice of mindful movement, posture, and balance will lead to a natural grace that becomes part of your everyday life. Physical grace is the outward expression of inner harmony. When you cultivate peace, confidence, and mindfulness within, it naturally reflects in your physical presence.

Summary:

This chapter began with strategies for building stamina, which involves consistent aerobic exercises and balanced nutrition to sustain energy over prolonged periods. Strengthening muscles focuses on targeted resistance training to increase muscle mass and power. Endurance training builds on this by enhancing your ability to perform extended physical activities without fatigue. Flexibility exercises improve the range of motion and prevent injuries while overcoming physical weakness involves addressing and strengthening areas of vulnerability. Balancing strength and agility ensures that physical power is complemented by swift, coordinated movements.

Nature walks and the power of posture highlights the importance of natural environments and correct alignment in physical well-being. Restorative practices and resilience training emphasise recovery and mental toughness, crucial for sustaining physical efforts. Enhancing the immune system and mastering balance further support overall health and functional ability. Physical courage encourages pushing boundaries while listening to the body ensures you respect limits and prevent overtraining. Finally, streamlining physical exercise and cultivating physical grace integrate efficient routines and elegant movements, enhancing both performance and personal expression.

Part II – AWAKE

Chapter 4 – The Power of the Mind

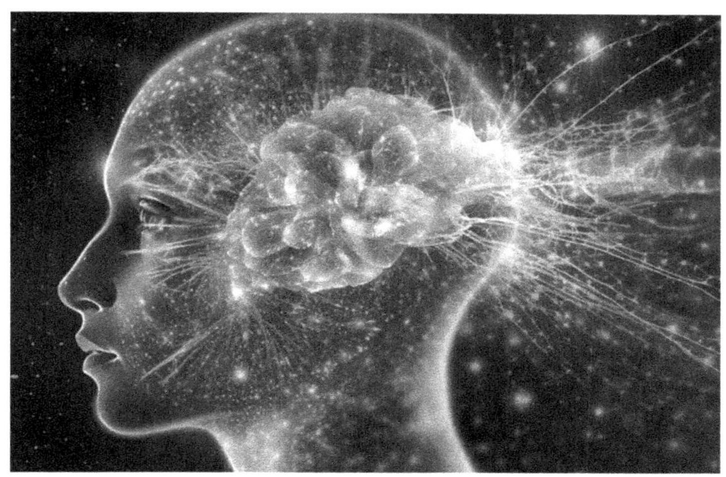

Source: neurosciencenews.com

> *"Go on saying, I am free. Never mind if the next moment delusion comes and says, I am bound. Dehypnotise the whole thing."*
>
> *–Swami Vivekananda*

This quote encourages us to affirm our freedom and true nature despite challenges or negative thoughts that might arise. When you say, "I am free," you're reminding yourselves of your inner strength and potential. Even if doubts or feelings of being trapped surface, it's important to stay committed to this positive affirmation. The term "dehypnotise" suggests that you should free yourselves from the false beliefs or limitations that your mind might impose. Just as someone might be hypnotised into thinking you're bound, you can also become trapped by your doubts. By repeatedly affirming your freedom and potential, you can overcome these mental barriers and align yourselves with your true capabilities. The key is persistence (keeping your focus on your inner freedom despite any temporary setbacks or negative thoughts).

Understanding the Mind:

Understanding the mind is a journey into the very essence of your being, an exploration that reveals not only our nature but also the universal principles that govern all life. The mind, in its true nature, is a reflection of the infinite and eternal reality. To understand it, we must delve deeper than mere surface-level observations and grasp the fundamental truths that lie beneath our thoughts and emotions. At its core, the mind is a vast and dynamic field of consciousness. It is often compared to an ocean, with thoughts and feelings resembling the waves that rise and fall upon its surface. Just as the ocean remains unchanged regardless of

the turbulence on its surface, the mind's true nature remains constant amidst the shifting currents of our daily experiences. This distinction between the surface and the deeper layers of the mind is crucial in understanding its true essence.

One of the central aspects of the mind is its dual nature. On one hand, it is a tool of perception and reasoning, capable of discerning and analysing the world around us. On the other hand, it is also a source of illusions and distractions, often leading us away from our true purpose and inner peace. The mind's ability to create both clarity and confusion highlights the need for disciplined self-awareness and control. By learning to master the fluctuations of our thoughts and emotions, we can begin to align ourselves with a higher state of consciousness.

To understand the mind fully, one must recognise the importance of self-knowledge and inner reflection. Understanding the mind involves recognising the interconnectedness of all existence. The mind is not an isolated entity but is intricately connected to the broader universe. Our thoughts and actions have a ripple effect that influences not only our own lives but also the lives of those around us. This awareness fosters a sense of unity and compassion, encouraging us to act with greater mindfulness and consideration for others.

It is about realising our potential and recognising the boundless nature of our consciousness. It is a process of inner exploration that leads to greater self-awareness, harmony, and ultimately, a profound connection with the universal truths that govern all existence.

Controlling Thoughts:

Controlling thoughts involves developing the ability to direct and manage our mental processes rather than being passively influenced by them. This practice is essential for personal growth, emotional well-being, and overall effectiveness in life.

Our thoughts often act like a torrent of water, flowing in various directions and sometimes overwhelming us with their intensity. They can be driven by external stimuli, internal desires, or deep-seated fears. To control our thoughts, we must first recognise that they are not necessarily reflective of our true selves. Instead, they are transient events within the mind that can be shaped and directed through conscious effort.

The first step in controlling thoughts is cultivating awareness. By observing our thoughts without judgement, we become more aware of their patterns and origins. This mindfulness allows us to identify recurring themes or negative thought patterns that may be influencing our behaviour and emotions. Awareness is key to gaining control because it breaks the automatic and unconscious cycle of thinking, allowing us to choose how we respond. Once we have developed awareness, the next step is to practice redirecting our thoughts. This can be achieved through various techniques such as focusing on positive affirmations, and visualisations, or engaging in activities that bring joy and fulfilment. For instance, if negative or anxious thoughts begin to dominate, consciously shifting attention to a positive goal or a calming image can help restore balance and focus.

It is also important to address the root causes of persistent or troubling thoughts. Often, these thoughts are a manifestation of deeper issues such as unresolved conflicts or unmet needs. Adopting a balanced lifestyle that includes physical exercise, healthy nutrition, and adequate rest supports mental well-being and enhances our ability to control thoughts. When the body is healthy and energised, the mind is better equipped to manage and direct its processes effectively.

The Power of Belief:

Beliefs act as the lenses through which we perceive the world and determine our experiences. They are not mere thoughts but deeply ingrained convictions that guide our actions, affect our emotions, and define our identity. Beliefs shape our expectations, behaviours, and interactions with the world.

The power of belief is evident in various aspects of life. Considering health, studies have shown that individuals who maintain positive beliefs about their well-being are more likely to experience improved health outcomes. The placebo effect, where patients experience real improvements in their condition due to their belief in the treatment, is a striking example of how belief can influence physical health. Considering personal growth, belief plays a crucial role in overcoming challenges and achieving success. A person who believes in their potential is more likely to set ambitious goals, embrace challenges, and persist through difficulties.

Beliefs also shape our relationships and interactions with others. Our beliefs about ourselves and others influence how we communicate, connect, and collaborate. For example, believing in the goodness of others can lead to more trusting and supportive relationships, while mistrust can create barriers and conflict.

Changing our beliefs can lead to transformative shifts in our lives. By challenging and reshaping limiting or negative beliefs, we open ourselves up to new possibilities and experiences. This process often involves self-reflection, questioning ingrained assumptions, and adopting new perspectives. Through this conscious effort, we can align our beliefs with our aspirations and values, leading to a more fulfilling and authentic life.

The power of belief extends beyond the individual to influence collective outcomes. Shared beliefs within communities or organisations can drive collective actions and shape societal norms. For instance, a community that believes in the importance of environmental conservation may work together to implement sustainable practices and advocate for policy changes, leading to a positive impact on the environment.

Positive Affirmations:

Positive affirmations are powerful tools for shaping our mindset and influencing our reality. They are concise, affirmative statements designed to reinforce positive beliefs and attitudes. By regularly repeating these affirmations, we can rewire our thought patterns, boost self-esteem, and manifest our goals.

Affirmations should be clear and specific to be effective. Rather than vague statements like "I am successful," use specific affirmations such as "I am confidently handling my work tasks and achieving my career goals." This precision helps direct your focus and intention. Frame affirmations in the present tense as if the desired outcome is already happening. For instance, say "I am healthy and energetic" rather than "I will be healthy and energetic." This approach helps to create a sense of immediacy and internalise the affirmation.

Use positive language to affirm what you want, rather than what you don't want. For example, instead of saying "I am not stressed," say "I am calm and relaxed." Positive language helps to foster a constructive mindset. Repetition is key to reinforcing affirmations. Repeat them daily, ideally in the morning or before bed, to embed them deeply into your subconscious mind. Regular practice helps to shift your mindset over time. Combine affirmations with visualisation techniques. As you repeat your affirmations, visualise yourself experiencing the desired outcome. This enhances the emotional impact and makes the affirmation more vivid and compelling.

Engage emotionally with your affirmations. Feel the positive emotions associated with the affirmation as you repeat it. This emotional connection strengthens the affirmation's impact and makes it more effective. Write your affirmations down and place them where you can see them regularly, such as on a vision board or sticky notes. Visual reminders help reinforce your commitment and keep your focus on your goals. Repeating positive affirmations helps build self-esteem by counteracting negative self-talk and reinforcing a positive self-image.

This boosts confidence and encourages a more positive outlook on life. Positive affirmations can reduce stress and anxiety by promoting a sense of calm and control. They shift focus away from negative thoughts and encourage a more optimistic perspective.

Affirmations can enhance motivation by keeping you focused on your goals and aspirations. They provide a daily reminder of your capabilities and the progress you are making. By aligning your thoughts and beliefs with your goals through affirmations, you can increase the likelihood of achieving them. Positive affirmations help to create a mental environment conducive to success and opportunities. Regular practice of positive affirmations fosters emotional resilience. They help you maintain a positive mindset even in challenging situations, enabling you to cope better with adversity. Positive affirmations can improve relationships by fostering a positive attitude and encouraging constructive communication. Believing in your worth and the value of others can lead to more harmonious interactions.

Mental Discipline:

Mental discipline is the ability to manage and direct one's thoughts, emotions, and actions to achieve specific goals and maintain well-being. It is fundamental to personal growth, productivity, and success. Cultivating mental discipline involves employing various techniques that enhance focus, resilience, and self-control.

By training the mind to stay present and manage distractions, practices like mindfulness and meditation can improve concentration, reduce stress, and foster a deeper awareness of one's thoughts and feelings. Effective time management is another essential aspect, involving the creation and adherence to schedules and deadlines. Self-monitoring also plays a vital role in mental discipline. Regularly assessing progress towards goals and evaluating behaviours allows for continuous improvement and accountability. Positive reinforcement further strengthens commitment by rewarding milestones and encouraging continued effort. Visualisation, where one mentally imagines achieving goals, reinforces commitment and prepares the mind for future challenges. Establishing a consistent daily routine contributes to mental discipline by providing structure and reinforcing productive habits. Additionally, maintaining a healthy lifestyle through adequate sleep, regular exercise and a balanced diet supports cognitive function and emotional stability, enhancing overall mental clarity.

The benefits of mental discipline are profound. Enhanced focus and productivity result from improved concentration and reduced procrastination. Increased resilience helps individuals cope with challenges and adapt to setbacks. Achieving long-term goals becomes more feasible with sustained discipline, and greater self-control supports the avoidance of distractions and adherence to healthy habits.

Overcoming Self-doubt:

Self-doubt, that nagging feeling of uncertainty about one's abilities and decisions, can significantly hinder progress and erode self-confidence. Addressing and overcoming self-doubt involves a multifaceted approach that includes understanding its origins, developing self-awareness, and employing strategies to build confidence and resilience.

The first step in overcoming self-doubt is to understand its origins. Self-doubt often stems from past experiences, societal expectations, or internalised fears. Reflecting on the root causes of self-doubt can provide insights into its triggers and help address the underlying issues.

Developing self-awareness is another crucial aspect of overcoming self-doubt. By actively observing and questioning negative thoughts, individuals can begin to challenge and reframe them. Journaling can be a useful tool for this process, allowing individuals to record and analyse their thoughts and feelings. This practice helps to identify recurring patterns of self-doubt and provides an opportunity to counteract them with more positive and realistic affirmations. Building self-confidence is essential in overcoming self-doubt. Setting small, achievable goals and celebrating each success, no matter how minor helps to build a sense of accomplishment and reinforce self-belief. Positive affirmations can also play a significant role. Repeating affirmations that focus on strengths and achievements helps to shift the mindset from one of doubt to one of confidence and optimism.

Engaging in self-care and surrounding oneself with supportive individuals can further boost confidence. Taking care of physical health through exercise, proper nutrition, and adequate rest enhances overall well-being and mental clarity. Additionally, surrounding oneself with a supportive network of friends, family, or mentors provides encouragement and constructive feedback, reinforcing positive self-perceptions. Professionals can offer guidance and techniques tailored to individual needs, helping to address deep-seated issues and develop strategies for building self-confidence.

Understanding that skills and abilities can be developed through effort and learning helps to reframe failures as opportunities for growth rather than as reflections of inadequacy. This mindset encourages resilience and persistence, allowing individuals to approach challenges with a more positive and proactive attitude.

Inner Strength:

Inner strength is a vital yet often intangible quality that enables individuals to persevere through adversity and emerge stronger from life's trials. Unlike external achievements or material successes, inner strength is an internal reservoir of fortitude, resilience, and self-belief that drives individuals to overcome challenges and maintain their integrity under pressure.

Developing inner strength begins with fostering self-awareness. This involves a deep understanding of one's values, passions, and intrinsic motivations. Self-awareness allows individuals to align their actions with their core principles, providing a sense of purpose and direction even in difficult times. By regularly reflecting on their experiences and acknowledging their personal growth, individuals can build a strong foundation of self-assurance and clarity.

Emotional resilience is another key aspect of inner strength. It refers to the ability to bounce back from emotional setbacks and manage stress effectively. Cultivating emotional resilience involves practices such as mindfulness, which helps individuals remain present amid turmoil. Techniques like expressive writing also aid in processing emotions and gaining perspective, thereby strengthening one's capacity to handle emotional challenges.

Mental fortitude, the ability to stay focused and motivated despite obstacles, is crucial for inner strength. This quality requires a disciplined approach to goal-setting and perseverance. Setting achievable goals and maintaining a proactive mindset helps individuals stay committed to their objectives, even when progress is slow. Embracing a growth mindset, and believing that challenges are opportunities for learning and development, supports mental fortitude and fosters resilience.

Adaptability is a significant component of inner strength. Life is full of unexpected changes and uncertainties, and the ability to adapt is essential for navigating these fluctuations. Embracing change with an open mind and a flexible attitude allows individuals to respond effectively to new circumstances. Viewing change as a chance for growth rather than a setback enhances one's capacity to maintain inner strength. Self-care practices also play a crucial role in reinforcing inner strength. Taking time to nurture one's physical, emotional, and mental well-being supports overall resilience. Activities such as regular physical exercise, balanced nutrition, and sufficient rest help maintain energy levels and mental clarity. Engaging in hobbies, spending time with supportive individuals, and practising relaxation techniques further bolster one's ability to cope with stress and maintain a positive outlook.

Self-knowledge:

Self-knowledge is the understanding of one's own character, values, strengths, and weaknesses and desires. Unlike external knowledge or academic learning, self-knowledge delves deeply into personal insight and self-awareness, guiding individuals in making informed decisions and fostering personal growth. It is a crucial component of living a fulfilling life and achieving a sense of authenticity and purpose.

The journey to self-knowledge begins with introspection. Introspection involves reflecting on one's thoughts, feelings, and behaviours to gain a deeper understanding of oneself. This process requires asking insightful questions about what drives one's actions, what values are held dear, and how one reacts to various situations. By honestly examining past experiences and current motivations, individuals can uncover patterns and insights that reveal their true selves.

Understanding one's strengths and weaknesses is a significant aspect of self-knowledge. Recognising strengths allows individuals to leverage their unique abilities and talents, leading to increased confidence and effectiveness in various aspects of life. Conversely, acknowledging weaknesses provides opportunities for growth and development. This awareness helps in setting realistic goals, seeking relevant opportunities for improvement, and building resilience against challenges. Self-knowledge also involves understanding personal values and priorities. Values are the guiding principles that influence decision-making and behaviour. By identifying what truly matters to them, individuals can make choices that align with their core beliefs and lead to greater satisfaction and authenticity. This alignment ensures that actions and decisions are consistent with one's true self, rather than being influenced by external pressures or societal expectations.

Another important element of self-knowledge is emotional awareness. Being in tune with one's emotions and understanding how they impact thoughts and behaviour is crucial for personal growth. Emotional awareness enables individuals to manage their responses effectively, communicate more empathetically, and build healthier relationships. It also contributes to better stress management and overall emotional well-being. Engaging in self-discovery practices can enhance self-knowledge. Personality assessments, while not definitive, offer frameworks for understanding one's traits and preferences.

Mastering Emotions:

Mastering emotions involves developing the ability to understand, manage, and utilise one's emotional responses effectively. Unlike merely experiencing or reacting to emotions, mastering them means gaining control over how emotions influence behaviour and decision-making, leading to a more balanced and purposeful life.

The first step in mastering emotions is recognising and acknowledging them. Emotional awareness involves identifying what you are feeling and understanding the sources and triggers of these emotions. This process begins with mindfulness, where you focus on the present moment and observe your emotional responses without judgement. By paying attention to your emotional state, you can gain insights into how different situations affect you and why certain emotions arise. Once you have identified your emotions, the next step is to understand their underlying causes. Emotions are often signals that reflect deeper needs or unresolved issues. For example, feeling anxious might indicate a fear of failure, while anger could be a response to perceived injustice. Exploring these underlying causes helps you address the root issues rather than just managing surface-level emotions. Techniques such as journaling or talking with a therapist can aid in uncovering these deeper emotional drivers. Managing emotions effectively requires developing strategies to regulate and respond to them constructively.

One key technique is cognitive restructuring, which involves changing the way you think about a situation to alter your emotional response. For instance, if you are feeling overwhelmed by a challenging task, reframing it as an opportunity for growth rather than a threat can reduce anxiety and increase motivation. Another important aspect of emotional mastery is practising emotional resilience. This involves building the ability to bounce back from emotional setbacks and maintain equilibrium in the face of adversity. Techniques such as stress management, relaxation exercises, and maintaining a balanced lifestyle contribute to emotional resilience. Regular physical activity, healthy eating, and sufficient rest play crucial roles in maintaining emotional balance and enhancing overall well-being. Effective communication is also a vital component of mastering emotions. Being able to express your feelings clearly and assertively helps in managing emotional interactions with others. Active listening and empathy are key skills in this regard, as they enable you to understand others' perspectives and respond in a way that fosters constructive dialogue and emotional support.

Moreover, setting boundaries is essential for emotional mastery. Boundaries help protect your emotional well-being by defining limits on how others can affect you. Learning to assert your needs and saying no when necessary ensures that you maintain control over your emotional state and prevent undue stress or discomfort. Developing emotional intelligence further supports emotional mastery. Emotional intelligence involves recognising, understanding, and managing both your own emotions and those of others. By enhancing emotional intelligence, you improve your ability to navigate complex social interactions, resolve conflicts, and build meaningful relationships.

Harmony of Thought and Action:

Achieving harmony between thought and action is crucial for living a balanced and purposeful life. This alignment means that one's actions are consistent with their beliefs, values and intentions, leading to greater personal satisfaction and effectiveness in achieving goals. When thought and action are in harmony, individuals experience a sense of integrity and coherence that enhances overall well-being and productivity.

The journey toward harmony begins with clarity of thought. Clear thinking involves understanding and articulating one's values, goals, and intentions. This process requires self-reflection and mindfulness to identify what is genuinely important and to ensure that these values are at the core of decision-making. By defining clear objectives and aligning them with personal values, you can create a roadmap for your actions that reflects your true intentions.

The next step is to translate these clear thoughts into concrete actions. This involves setting actionable goals and developing a plan to achieve them. Breaking down larger goals into smaller, manageable tasks ensures that each action is purposeful and aligned with the overall vision. Regularly reviewing and adjusting this plan helps to maintain focus and adapt to any changes, ensuring that actions remain aligned with evolving thoughts and circumstances. Consistency between thought and action requires self-discipline and commitment. Self-discipline involves adhering to one's plan and making choices that support the desired outcomes, even when faced with distractions or challenges. Building self-discipline involves creating habits and routines that reinforce alignment between thought and action. For example, setting regular times for reflection, goal-setting, and review helps to maintain focus and ensure that actions are consistently aligned with intentions.

Another key aspect of achieving harmony is managing internal conflicts. Sometimes, individuals may experience discrepancies between their thoughts and actions due to internal conflicts or competing priorities. Resolving these conflicts involves addressing any underlying issues and making conscious choices that align with one's core values and goals. Techniques such as cognitive restructuring and emotional regulation can help in resolving internal conflicts and ensuring that actions are consistent with one's true self. Effective communication is also crucial for maintaining harmony between thought and action. Clear communication with others about one's goals and intentions fosters mutual understanding and support. It helps to set expectations and create an environment that encourages alignment between personal actions and broader objectives.

Seeking feedback and being open to growth and change contribute to achieving harmony. Feedback from trusted sources provides valuable insights into how well one's actions align with their thoughts and intentions. Being open to this feedback and willing to make adjustments ensures continuous improvement and maintains the alignment between thought and action.

The harmony of thought and action fosters a sense of fulfilment and authenticity. When individuals' actions are congruent with their thoughts and values, they experience greater satisfaction and effectiveness in their endeavours.

Impact of Thought on Health:

The impact of thoughts on both mental and physical health is profound and multifaceted. Thoughts shape our perception of reality, influence our emotional state, and ultimately affect our overall well-being. Understanding this connection highlights the importance of cultivating a positive and constructive thought pattern to enhance both mental and physical health. Thoughts play a significant role in shaping emotional experiences. Positive thoughts can foster feelings of joy, satisfaction, and resilience, while negative or distressing thoughts often lead to feelings of anxiety, sadness, or frustration. The cognitive appraisal of situations (how we interpret and evaluate them) directly influences our emotional reactions. For example, viewing a challenging situation as an opportunity for growth rather than a threat can lead to a more constructive emotional response and better coping strategies.

The connection between thoughts and mental health is well-documented. Persistent negative thinking patterns, such as rumination or self-criticism, are closely linked to various mental health issues, including depression and anxiety. These negative thought patterns can create a cycle of distress, where negative emotions reinforce pessimistic thoughts, leading to further emotional and psychological strain. Cognitive-behavioural therapy (CBT) and other therapeutic approaches aim to break this cycle by helping individuals recognise and reframe negative thought patterns, thereby improving mental health outcomes.

On a physiological level, thoughts also influence physical health. The mind-body connection is evident in how stress and anxiety manifest physically. Chronic stress, driven by negative or persistent worrying thoughts, can activate the body's stress response system, leading to the release of stress hormones such as cortisol. Prolonged exposure to elevated cortisol levels can contribute to a range of health problems, including weakened immune function, digestive issues, cardiovascular disease, and chronic inflammation.

Conversely, positive thinking and mental practices such as mindfulness and relaxation techniques have been shown to have beneficial effects on physical health. Engaging in activities that promote relaxation and reduce stress, such as meditation, deep breathing exercises, or progressive muscle relaxation, can help lower cortisol levels and enhance overall physical well-being. Studies have demonstrated that individuals who practice mindfulness report lower levels of stress, improved immune function, and better management of chronic conditions. Thoughts and beliefs about one's health can influence health behaviours and outcomes. Individuals who hold positive beliefs about their ability to manage their health are more likely to engage in health-promoting behaviours, such as regular exercise, balanced nutrition, and adherence to medical advice. Conversely, negative beliefs about health can lead to avoidance of healthy behaviours and increased risk of illness.

Creative Thinking:

Creative thinking is the process of generating new, original ideas or concepts that offer novel solutions to problems or open up new possibilities. It transcends traditional problem-solving methods by allowing individuals to think outside conventional boundaries and explore innovative approaches. Cultivating creative thinking involves fostering a mindset that embraces curiosity, experimentation, and flexibility. At the heart of creative thinking is the ability to make connections between seemingly unrelated ideas or concepts. This process, often referred to as associative thinking, involves drawing parallels between different fields, experiences, or perspectives to spark innovative ideas. For example, an individual might combine knowledge from technology and art to develop a new form of interactive media. By encouraging diverse inputs and perspectives, creative thinking breaks free from linear patterns and opens up new avenues for exploration.

Another key aspect of creative thinking is the willingness to take risks and embrace failure as a learning opportunity. Creative endeavours often involve experimentation and trial and error, where not every idea will succeed. A growth mindset, which views failures as stepping stones to improvement, is essential for fostering creativity. By viewing setbacks as part of the learning process, individuals can persist in their creative pursuits and refine their ideas based on feedback and experience.

Creating an environment that supports creativity also plays a crucial role. A stimulating and flexible environment encourages the free flow of ideas and reduces constraints that might stifle creativity. This can be achieved by providing spaces that are physically inspiring and mentally open, where brainstorming and unconventional thinking are encouraged. An environment that values diverse viewpoints and fosters collaboration further enhances creative thinking, as it allows for the cross-pollination of ideas and approaches.

Techniques such as brainstorming, mind mapping, and lateral thinking can also facilitate creative thought. Brainstorming sessions, where ideas are generated without immediate judgement, allow for a wide range of possibilities to be explored. Mind mapping helps in organising and visually connecting different ideas, making it easier to see relationships and develop new insights. Lateral thinking techniques, such as deliberately challenging assumptions or looking at a problem from different angles, can also uncover innovative solutions that might not be apparent through conventional reasoning.

Including regular practices that stimulate creativity can further enhance one's ability to think creatively. Engaging in activities such as reading widely, exploring new hobbies, and seeking out new experiences can provide fresh perspectives and inspire innovative thinking. Creativity is often nurtured by stepping outside of one's comfort zone and exposing oneself to diverse inputs and experiences. Fostering an attitude of curiosity and questioning is fundamental to creative thinking. Asking "what if" questions and exploring hypothetical scenarios can lead to new ideas and solutions. This inquisitive approach encourages deeper exploration and understanding, paving the way for creative breakthroughs.

Developing Intuition:

Developing intuition involves improving the ability to understand or know something without the need for conscious reasoning. It is often described as a "gut feeling" or an innate sense of understanding that guides decision-making and problem-solving. Cultivating intuition requires a combination of self-awareness, reflection, and experiential learning. Intuition draws from a deep reservoir of knowledge and experiences accumulated over time. It operates on the subconscious mind, which processes vast amounts of information that may not be immediately accessible through rational thought. To develop intuition, individuals must first become more attuned to their inner thoughts and feelings. Practices such as mindfulness and meditation can enhance this self-awareness by helping individuals tune into their internal states and recognise subtle cues that might otherwise be overlooked.

Regularly reflecting on past experiences and decisions helps individuals recognise patterns and gain insights into how intuitive judgements have played a role in their lives. This reflection involves examining situations where intuition guided successful outcomes as well as instances where it did not. By analysing these experiences, individuals can learn to discern which intuitive signals are reliable and which may need further scrutiny. Exposure to diverse experiences and challenges also contributes to developing intuition. Engaging in a variety of activities, exploring different fields, and tackling new problems broadens one's knowledge base and enriches the subconscious mind. As individuals encounter and navigate various situations, they build a more nuanced understanding of patterns and relationships, which enhances their intuitive abilities.

For example, someone who frequently engages in creative problem-solving may develop a sharper sense of intuition related to innovative solutions. Training and practice can further refine intuition.

Techniques such as journaling can be useful for tracking intuitive insights and evaluating their accuracy over time. Keeping a record of intuitive decisions and their outcomes allows individuals to identify trends and improve their ability to trust their instincts. Additionally, participating in exercises that challenge cognitive and emotional processing, such as scenario planning or role-playing, can strengthen intuitive skills by simulating real-world decision-making. Listening to and trusting one's intuition is crucial for its development. Often, individuals may second-guess or dismiss their intuitive feelings in favour of rational analysis. Building confidence in one's intuition involves acknowledging and validating these feelings, especially when they align with past experiences and knowledge.

Mind as a Tool:

The mind as a tool can be significantly enhanced through a variety of powerful techniques, each offering distinct benefits for cognitive function, emotional regulation, and personal effectiveness. One such technique is mindfulness meditation, which involves focusing attention on the present moment while observing thoughts and feelings without judgement. Regular practice of mindfulness can lead to improved emotional regulation, reduced stress, and heightened awareness. To start, find a quiet space, sit comfortably, and focus on your breath. As thoughts arise, gently guide your attention back to your breathing, gradually increasing the duration of your practice.

Cognitive restructuring, also known as cognitive reframing, is a technique focused on changing negative thought patterns. By identifying and reframing irrational or unproductive thoughts, individuals can shift to a more positive and constructive mindset.

For instance, if you catch yourself thinking, "I always fail," reframe it to, "I may face challenges, but I learn and improve with each experience." This technique promotes emotional resilience and more effective problem-solving by fostering a growth-oriented perspective.

Goal-setting, coupled with strategic planning, leverages the mind's focus and discipline. Setting clear, actionable goals and breaking them into smaller, manageable tasks directs mental energy effectively. This approach enhances motivation and provides a clear path to achievement. Start by defining specific, measurable goals and outlining the steps needed to reach them. Regularly review and adjust your plan as necessary to stay on track and maintain focus. Physical exercise is another effective technique for enhancing mental function and clarity. Exercise increases blood flow to the brain, boosts cognitive function, and reduces stress. Including activities such as walking, jogging, or yoga in your routine can improve mental sharpness and overall well-being.

Another technique is creative expression through activities like drawing, painting, or music. Creative outlets can stimulate the mind and enhance problem-solving skills. Engaging in creative activities allows for the exploration of new perspectives and ideas, fostering cognitive flexibility. Engaging in regular learning and intellectual challenges, such as puzzles, reading, or new skills acquisition, keeps the mind active and sharp. Continuous mental stimulation promotes cognitive growth and resilience.

The Power of Imagination:

The power of imagination is a remarkable asset that can transform thoughts into reality and unlock creative potential. By harnessing this innate capability, individuals can enhance problem-solving skills, foster innovation, and achieve personal goals. Several techniques can amplify the effectiveness of imagination, each offering unique benefits that contribute to personal and professional growth.

Another valuable technique is guided imagery, which involves using narrative or audio prompts to stimulate the imagination. Guided imagery often includes scripts or recordings that lead individuals through specific scenarios, helping them explore different aspects of a situation or goal. This technique is beneficial for reducing stress, enhancing relaxation, and increasing mental clarity. To use guided imagery, find a quiet space, listen to a guided meditation or script, and follow the narrative to explore various mental scenarios.

Creative brainstorming is a technique that leverages imagination to generate a wide range of ideas and solutions. This process involves freely and openly generating ideas without immediate judgement, allowing the mind to explore unconventional and innovative concepts. Brainstorming sessions can be conducted individually or in groups, encouraging the free flow of ideas and the exploration of diverse perspectives. To effectively brainstorm, create a supportive environment where all ideas are welcomed, and use techniques like mind mapping or free writing to capture and organise thoughts.

Mind mapping is another technique that uses imagination to visually organise and explore ideas. By creating a visual representation of thoughts and concepts, individuals can see connections and relationships that might not be immediately apparent through linear thinking. Mind mapping involves placing a central idea in the centre of a page and branching out with related concepts and ideas. This technique enhances creative problem-solving by allowing the mind to explore multiple dimensions of a topic or challenge. Engaging in imaginative play or creative hobbies, such as drawing, writing fiction, or role-playing, stimulates the mind and nurtures creativity. These activities provide a space for exploring new ideas, experimenting with different perspectives, and expressing oneself in novel ways.

Immersing oneself in creative pursuits can boost mental flexibility, foster innovation, and provide a sense of fulfilment and joy. Techniques such as visualisation, guided imagery, creative brainstorming, mind mapping, and engaging in imaginative play harness the power of imagination to foster personal and professional growth. Each technique offers specific benefits, from enhancing motivation and confidence to improving problem-solving skills and nurturing creativity.

The Mind and Body Connection:

The connection between mind and body is a profound and dynamic relationship that profoundly impacts overall health and well-being. Understanding and optimising this connection can lead to improved physical health, emotional balance, and mental clarity. Several effective techniques can help enhance the harmony between the mind and body, each offering distinct benefits.

One powerful technique for strengthening the mind-body connection is mindfulness meditation. Yoga is another technique that integrates the mind and body through physical movement and breath control. This ancient practice combines postures, breathing exercises, and meditation to promote physical flexibility and mental strength. The mindful movement and deep breathing involved in yoga help to harmonise the body's physiological processes with mental and emotional states, leading to reduced stress and enhanced overall health. Regular yoga practice can improve posture, increase energy levels, and support mental clarity.

Progressive muscle relaxation (PMR) is a technique designed to enhance the mind-body connection by reducing physical tension and promoting relaxation. PMR involves systematically tensing and then relaxing different muscle groups, which helps to increase awareness of bodily sensations and alleviate stress. By practising PMR regularly, individuals can learn to identify and release areas of tension, leading to improved physical comfort and a more relaxed state of mind. To practise PMR, find a quiet space, focus on one muscle group at a time, tense the muscles for a few seconds, and then release the tension slowly.

Another effective method is guided imagery, which uses the power of the mind to influence physical health. Guided imagery involves visualising peaceful and healing scenarios, which can help reduce stress and promote physical relaxation. This technique leverages the mind's ability to impact the body's physiological responses, such as lowering heart rate and easing muscle tension. To use guided imagery, find a comfortable position, close your eyes, and visualise a calming scene or place, allowing yourself to fully immerse in the sensory experience. Techniques such as mindfulness meditation, yoga, progressive muscle relaxation, guided imagery, and maintaining a balanced lifestyle all contribute to strengthening the connection between the mind and body. Each technique offers specific benefits, including reduced stress, improved physical health, and enhanced mental clarity.

Transcending the Ego:

Transcending the ego involves moving beyond the self-centred aspects of our identity to experience a deeper sense of connection and unity with the world. This journey toward transcending the ego is often described as a path to greater self-awareness and inner peace, where one aligns with a more expansive and less fragmented sense of self. Several powerful techniques and practices can facilitate this transformative process, each offering unique benefits for personal growth and spiritual development.

Self-inquiry, as a technique, involves exploring the fundamental question, "Who am I?" This introspective practice aims to uncover the true self beyond the ego's constructs and illusions. By questioning the nature of one's identity and examining the source of personal thoughts and beliefs, individuals can gain insight into the deeper essence of their being. Self-inquiry encourages the realisation that the ego is not the core of one's existence but rather a transient aspect of the self. To engage in self-inquiry, set aside quiet time for reflection, asking yourself questions like, "What is the source of my thoughts?" and "Who am I beyond my roles and experiences?"

Another effective method is the practice of compassion and empathy. By extending compassion to others and deeply understanding their perspectives, individuals can shift focus away from their ego and connect with a broader, more inclusive sense of self. Compassionate practices help dissolve the boundaries between self and others, fostering a sense of interconnectedness and shared humanity.

Spiritual practices such as contemplation and prayer can also support the transcendence of the ego. These practices often involve connecting with a higher power or universal consciousness, which helps individuals move beyond the confines of their self. Engaging in creative expression can facilitate ego transcendence by allowing individuals to tap into a state of flow and lose the sense of self-consciousness. Activities such as art, music, or writing can help bypass the ego's limitations and connect with a deeper source of creativity and inspiration.

Summary:

In this chapter, we explore the capabilities of the mind and its transformative potential. It begins with understanding the mind's intricate functions and moves on to techniques for controlling thoughts and harnessing the power of belief and positive affirmations. Mental discipline is emphasised as a foundation for overcoming self-doubt and building inner strength. The chapter delves into self-knowledge and mastering emotions, promoting harmony between thought and action. It discusses the significant impact of thoughts on health and the importance of mental clarity.

Creative thinking and intuition are highlighted as tools for innovation, while the mind is recognised as a powerful instrument for achieving goals. The power of imagination and the mind-body connection is examined, culminating in the concept of transcending the ego to achieve a greater sense of unity and self-awareness. Through these practices, individuals can enhance their well-being and personal growth.

Chapter 5 – Spiritual Awakening

Source: medium.com

"There is no other spiritual teacher than your own soul."
–Swami Vivekananda

The true guide to spiritual growth and understanding lies within ourselves. Instead of relying on external teachers or sources, it suggests that our soul, or inner self, holds the wisdom we seek. Every person has an innate connection to their higher self, and by listening to our intuition and inner voice, we can find clarity, purpose, and peace. The soul understands our deepest desires, struggles, and lessons better than anyone else. When we tune into this inner guidance, we often find answers that resonate more deeply than external advice.

This doesn't mean we shouldn't learn from others, but rather that the ultimate authority on our spiritual path comes from within.

Understanding the Soul:

Understanding the soul is the foundation of spiritual awakening. The soul represents the eternal essence of who we are, beyond the physical body and ego-driven mind. It is the divine spark within us, connected to a higher consciousness, and the source of our deepest sense of purpose, love, and wisdom. While the concept of the soul can be abstract, integrating practices that help you connect with this inner essence can lead to profound spiritual growth, a deeper sense of meaning, and a more peaceful existence.

The soul is often described as the true self, distinct from the transient aspects of our identity such as the physical body, emotions, and thoughts. Unlike the ego, which is concerned with personal survival, desires, and fears, the soul is concerned with the greater good, universal truths, and the collective well-being of all. It is timeless and unchanging, serving as a constant presence throughout the various experiences of life.

Understanding the soul begins with the recognition that we are more than our physical existence. While the body and mind are essential aspects of our experience, they are not the entirety of who we are. The soul transcends the limitations of the material world and connects us to something far greater: a universal consciousness or divine presence.

Through meditation, quieting the mind and turning your attention inward, you can begin to experience the stillness and presence of your soul. A meditation practice focused on the inner self involves sitting in silence, closing your eyes, and directing your awareness to the centre of your being. Feel the energy within you, beyond thoughts and emotions, and recognise this as the presence of your soul. Writing can be a powerful tool for self-discovery and soul connection. Ask yourself questions like "What is my true purpose?" or "What values guide my life?" and write down whatever comes to mind. Over time, patterns may emerge that reveal insights into your soul's nature and purpose.

Nature is a profound reflection of the soul's beauty and wisdom. Spending time in nature, whether walking in the woods, sitting by a river, or simply observing the sky, can help you connect with your soul. As you immerse yourself in nature's rhythms and cycles, you begin to sense the harmony and interconnectedness of all life, which mirrors the soul's essence. Engaging with spiritual texts and teachings can provide valuable insights into the nature of the soul. Whether through religious scriptures, philosophical works, or spiritual literature, studying these texts can offer guidance and understanding. Choose readings that resonate with your beliefs and explore them deeply, reflecting on how they apply to your spiritual journey.

The soul often communicates with us through intuition, a subtle inner knowing that transcends logic. Learning to trust and follow your intuition is a way of honouring your soul's guidance. Practice listening to that inner voice, especially when making decisions or facing challenges. The more you trust your intuition, the stronger your connection to your soul becomes. The soul is inherently compassionate and loving. By engaging in acts of kindness, you align yourself with your soul's true nature. Whether through small gestures of help, listening to someone in need, or simply being present for others, these acts cultivate a sense of unity and connection, reinforcing your soul's presence in your life.

Creativity is a powerful expression of the soul. Whether through art, music, writing, or any other forms of creative expression, allowing your creativity to flow freely can help you connect with your soul. This is not about producing something perfect but rather about expressing your true essence. Let go of judgements and simply create from the heart, allowing your soul to shine through your work. To deepen your understanding of the soul and maintain a strong connection, it's essential to establish a daily routine that nurtures your spiritual growth.

Begin your day with a few minutes of meditation focused on connecting with your soul. Set an intention to align with your highest self and carry that presence throughout your day. Each day, take a moment to express gratitude for the blessings in your life. Gratitude helps shift your focus from the material to the spiritual, fostering a deeper connection with your soul. Whether you're eating, working, or interacting with others, bring your awareness fully into the experience. Take a few minutes to reflect on your experiences. Consider how you connected with your soul throughout the day and what lessons you learned. This reflection reinforces your spiritual growth and sets the stage for deeper understanding. Dedicate time each week to studying spiritual texts or teachings. This practice keeps you connected to higher wisdom and provides ongoing guidance on your journey. Whether volunteering, helping a friend, or simply offering a kind word, these acts align you with your soul's compassionate nature.

When you connect with your soul, you experience a profound sense of inner peace that transcends the ups and downs of daily life. This peace comes from knowing that you are part of something greater and that your true essence is eternal. Understanding the soul helps you discover your true purpose in life. This sense of purpose brings meaning to your actions and guides you towards fulfilling your highest potential. As you deepen your connection with your soul, your intuition becomes more refined and trustworthy. You begin to rely on this inner guidance in all areas of your life. When you live from your soul, your relationships become more authentic and meaningful. Understanding the soul is the foundation of spiritual growth. It opens the door to higher states of consciousness, deeper insights, and a more profound connection with the divine.

Discovering the Purpose of Life:

The purpose of life is the search for meaning, direction, and fulfilment that transcends the daily grind and connects us to something greater than ourselves. Understanding the purpose of life is not about finding a single, definitive answer but rather about uncovering what resonates deeply with your soul and gives your life a sense of meaning and significance.

What is the purpose of life? The purpose of life can be seen as the underlying reason for our existence, a guiding principle that shapes our decisions, actions, and experiences. It is the driving force that propels us to grow, evolve, and contribute to the world in a meaningful way. While the specifics of life's purpose may vary from person to person, it often involves a combination of self-discovery, personal growth, service to others, and connection to a higher consciousness or divine presence. At its core, the purpose of life is about aligning with your true self, living authentically, and fulfilling your unique potential. It's about understanding who you are at the deepest level and expressing that essence in everything you do. Whether it's through your relationships, career, creative pursuits, or spiritual practices, living with purpose means infusing your life with intention and passion.

Discovering your purpose begins with self-reflection. Take time to explore your values, passions, and strengths. What brings you joy? What do you care deeply about? What are your natural talents and abilities? Reflect on your life experiences and consider how they have shaped you. Self-reflection helps you gain clarity about what truly matters to you and guides you toward your purpose. Start by asking yourself questions like "What do I want to be remembered for?" or "What impact do I want to make in the world?" Write down your thoughts without judgement or editing. Over time, patterns and themes may emerge that reveal insights into your purpose.

Pay attention to the activities, people, and experiences that energise you and make you feel alive. These are often clues to your purpose. Notice how you feel when you're engaged in different aspects of your life. When you're in alignment with your purpose, you'll feel a sense of flow and fulfilment. Many people find their purpose through acts of service. Helping others and contributing to the greater good can provide a deep sense of meaning and satisfaction. Volunteering, mentoring, or simply offering a kind word or gesture can connect you to your purpose by allowing you to make a positive difference in the world. Spiritual practices such as meditation, prayer, and contemplation can help you connect with your higher self and gain insights into your purpose. These practices quiet the mind and allow you to tune into your inner wisdom.

Your passions are often indicators of your purpose. Engage in activities that excite and inspire you. Whether it's art, music, writing, teaching, or another pursuit, following your passions can lead you to your purpose. Don't be afraid to experiment and try new things; sometimes your purpose emerges through exploration. If you're struggling to find your purpose, seek guidance from mentors, coaches, or spiritual teachers. Sometimes, an outside perspective can provide valuable insights and help you see things from a different angle. Don't hesitate to reach out for support as you navigate your journey. Your purpose is closely tied to authenticity. When you live in alignment with your true self, embracing your unique qualities, beliefs, and values, you naturally move closer to your purpose. Avoid conforming to societal expectations or trying to please others at the expense of your truth. Embrace who you are and let your authenticity guide you.

Living with purpose requires consistent effort and intention. To keep your purpose at the forefront of your life, establish a routine that supports your growth and fulfilment. Begin each day by setting an intention to live purposefully. This could be a simple affirmation like "I choose to live in alignment with my purpose today" or a specific goal that reflects your purpose. Approach your daily tasks with mindfulness and intention. Whether you're at work, with family, or engaging in personal activities, strive to do everything with purpose and presence. This transforms even mundane tasks into meaningful experiences.

Make time for regular reflection on your purpose. Weekly or monthly, check in with yourself to assess whether you're living in alignment with your purpose. Celebrate your progress and make adjustments as needed. Purposeful living involves continuous growth and learning. Seek out opportunities for personal and spiritual development. Take courses, read books, attend workshops, or engage in practices that help you expand your understanding of yourself and the world. Surround yourself with people who share your values and inspire you to live purposefully. These connections can provide support, encouragement, and opportunities to collaborate on meaningful projects. While pursuing your purpose is important, it's equally vital to balance it with rest and self-care. Avoid burnout by taking breaks, nurturing your well-being, and allowing yourself to recharge.

Living with purpose brings a deep sense of fulfilment and contentment. When your actions are aligned with your true self, you experience a sense of satisfaction that transcends material success. A strong sense of purpose helps you navigate challenges and setbacks with resilience. Knowing that your life has meaning gives you the strength to persevere in difficult times. Understanding your purpose provides clarity and focus, allowing you to prioritise what truly matters. Living with purpose enables you to make a positive impact on the world. Whether through your work, relationships, or acts of service, your purpose-driven actions contribute to the well-being of others. When you're aligned with your purpose, you experience inner peace and harmony. You no longer feel the need to chase external validation or approval.

The Power of Faith:

Faith is the unshakeable belief in something greater than ourselves, a guiding light that helps us navigate through life's challenges and uncertainties. The power of faith is not confined to religious contexts;

it extends to belief in oneself, in others, and the goodness of the world. This subtopic delves into the essence of faith, offering techniques and practices to harness its power for personal growth, resilience, and fulfilment.

Faith can be understood as a deep-seated trust and confidence in something that may not always be visible or tangible. It is the belief that there is a purpose behind every experience, even when it's not immediately clear. Faith allows us to move forward in life with a sense of hope, regardless of the obstacles we face. It transcends logic and reason, drawing on our inner strength and conviction. Faith is not about blind belief; it is about cultivating a strong inner foundation that supports us through life's ups and downs. Whether it's faith in a higher power, faith in the universe's unfolding plan, or faith in our abilities, this belief provides a sense of stability and purpose.

Faith grows through quiet contemplation and connection with your inner self. Regular meditation helps you tap into a deeper awareness and trust in the flow of life. During meditation, focus on the aspects of life that inspire faith, be it the beauty of nature, the kindness of others, or the wisdom of the universe. Reflection allows you to strengthen your faith by consciously acknowledging the positive aspects of your life and trusting in its continuity.

Use affirmations that reinforce your faith. Statements like "I trust in the process of life" or "I have faith that everything will work out for the best" help reprogram your mind to maintain a positive outlook. For those inclined towards spirituality, prayer can be a powerful practice for deepening faith. Praying for guidance, strength, or clarity reinforces your connection with a higher power and strengthens your trust in divine intervention. If prayer doesn't resonate with you, setting positive intentions can have a similar effect. Intend to approach each day with faith, trust, and confidence, and watch how your mindset shifts. This practice shifts your focus from fear and doubt to trust and abundance, reinforcing your faith in life's positive trajectory.

Engaging with stories and teachings that inspire faith can strengthen your belief system. Whether it's spiritual texts, biographies of resilient individuals, or uplifting literature, reading about others' experiences with faith can fortify your own. You can draw inspiration from how others have used faith to overcome adversity and achieve greatness. Serving others is a powerful way to cultivate faith. When you help others, you experience the interconnectedness of life and develop trust in the collective goodness of humanity. Acts of kindness and service remind you that despite life's challenges, there is always hope, and your contributions matter.

Surround yourself with people who share your values and beliefs. Being part of a community that encourages faith and positivity can provide emotional support and help you stay committed to your faith journey. Whether it's a religious group, a spiritual circle, or a supportive friendship network, having a community reinforces your belief in the power of faith. Faith often requires surrendering the need to control every aspect of life. Practice letting go of the things you cannot change and trusting that life will unfold as it should. This doesn't mean being passive, but rather, accepting that some things are beyond your influence and having faith that everything will work out in the end. Visualisation reinforces your belief that positive outcomes are possible, which in turn boosts your faith in the process.

Start your day with a practice that strengthens your faith. This could be a meditation session, prayer, or simply setting a positive intention for the day. Throughout the day, take moments to reconnect with your faith. When you encounter stress or doubt, pause, take a deep breath, and remind yourself of your faith. End your day by reflecting on how faith has played a role in your experiences. Acknowledge the moments when you felt guided, supported, or resilient. Once a week, dedicate time to a practice that renews your faith. This could involve attending a religious service, participating in a spiritual gathering, or spending time in nature. Regularly refreshing your connection with faith helps you stay aligned with your beliefs.

Faith gives you the strength to persevere through adversity. When you believe in a higher purpose or trust in the process, you can face challenges with greater courage and confidence. Faith provides a sense of calm and peace, even in difficult times. It allows you to let go of worry and fear, knowing that you are supported and guided. Faith gives your life a sense of meaning and purpose. When you believe in something greater than yourself, your actions are infused with intention and significance. It cultivates a positive mindset, helping you focus on the good in life rather than dwelling on the negative. This optimism attracts more positive experiences into your life. It also connects you to others, to your higher self, and to the universe. It fosters a sense of belonging and unity, reminding you that you are part of something greater.

Unity of All Beings:

The concept of unity of all beings, or the idea that all life is interconnected and part of a greater whole, is central to many spiritual traditions and philosophies. It's the recognition that every individual, creature, and element of the universe is intrinsically linked, forming a vast, harmonious network. This sense of oneness transcends superficial differences and highlights the shared essence that binds us all. Embracing this unity can lead to profound spiritual growth, inner peace, and a deepened sense of compassion and empathy.

Unity of all beings is the realisation that despite our unique identities and experiences, we are all expressions of the same universal consciousness. This perspective shifts the focus from individualism to a broader awareness of our collective existence. It encourages us to see ourselves not as isolated entities, but as integral parts of the larger fabric of life. This understanding fosters a sense of humility and interconnectedness. It reminds us that our actions have ripple effects on others and the world around us. When we embrace unity, we cultivate a mindset that prioritises harmony, cooperation, and mutual respect.

Compassion is the natural expression of recognising unity. By actively practising compassion in your daily life, you honour the interconnectedness of all beings. Whether through acts of kindness, empathy or simply being present for others, compassion bridges the gap between individuals and reinforces the sense of oneness. Make a conscious effort to treat others as extensions of yourself, understanding that their well-being is intertwined with your own. Spending time in nature can deepen your connection to the unity of all life. Nature operates in a harmonious balance, and observing this can help you feel more aligned with the larger ecosystem. Whether it's a walk in the forest, sitting by a river, or simply looking at the stars, allow nature to remind you of the beauty and interconnectedness of existence. Engage with nature mindfully, appreciating the intricate relationships between plants, animals, and the environment.

Communication is a powerful way to express and experience unity. Practice mindful listening and speaking, where your words and actions reflect a deep respect for the interconnectedness of life. When communicating, aim to bridge gaps, resolve conflicts, and foster understanding. This practice helps build connections that reinforce the idea that we are all part of the same universal family. Engaging in selfless service, or "seva," is a practical way to experience unity in action. By helping others without expecting anything in return, you align yourself with the principle of oneness. Selfless service reminds you that the happiness and well-being of others are just as important as your own. Reciting mantras that emphasise oneness, such as "Om," or phrases that invoke universal harmony, can help attune your mind to the vibration of unity. Prayer, too, can be a way to connect with the collective consciousness. Pray for the well-being of all beings, not just yourself or your immediate circle, and expand your awareness to include the entire universe.

Delving into spiritual texts that emphasise unity can provide profound insights and inspiration. Books, scriptures, or teachings from various traditions often explore the concept of oneness and how it can be applied in daily life. By studying these texts, you deepen your understanding of unity and find guidance on how to live in alignment with this principle. Cultivating gratitude for all forms of life reinforces the sense of unity. Express appreciation not only for human relationships but also for animals, plants, and the environment. Recognise that every being plays a role in the larger cosmic dance and acknowledge this interconnectedness.

When you consider the infinite expanse of space, the stars, and galaxies, you begin to see yourself as part of something much greater.

This contemplation can dissolve the boundaries of individuality and help you experience a sense of awe and connection to the entire cosmos. Art can be a medium to express and explore the unity of all beings. Whether through painting, music, dance, or writing, creative expression can help you tap into the collective consciousness. Create art that reflects the beauty of interconnectedness, or engage with others' creations that inspire a sense of oneness. Artistic expression allows you to transcend your ego and connect with the universal energy that flows through all life.

Begin your day with a meditation or prayer that focuses on unity. Set an intention to approach the day with an awareness of interconnectedness. This can help frame your actions and interactions in a way that honours the oneness of all beings. Make it a goal to perform at least one compassionate act each day. This could be as simple as a kind word, a helping hand, or a moment of mindful listening. These acts reinforce the unity of all life and create positive energy in your environment.

Incorporate time in nature into your daily or weekly routine. Whether it's a short walk or a longer retreat, being in nature helps you reconnect with the larger web of life. Use this time to reflect on the unity of all beings and how you are an integral part of the natural world. At the end of each day, reflect on the moments when you felt connected to others and the world around you. Acknowledge any instances where you acted from a place of unity, and consider how you can deepen this practice tomorrow. Engage in a weekly activity that strengthens your sense of oneness. This could be attending a group meditation, participating in community service, or simply spending time with loved ones. Regularly renewing your connection to unity helps keep it at the forefront of your consciousness.

Recognising the unity of all beings brings a profound sense of peace. When you see yourself as part of a larger whole, you can let go of the stresses of individualism and competition, finding solace in the interconnectedness of life. Unity fosters deep empathy and compassion. When you understand that others are not separate from you, their joy and suffering become your own, and you are naturally inclined to act with kindness and care. Embracing oneness provides a strong sense of purpose. Knowing that your actions impact the larger whole, you are motivated to live in a way that contributes positively to the world. Unity leads to more harmonious relationships. When you view others as extensions of yourself, conflicts are resolved with understanding and cooperation, rather than with division and competition. The practice of unity transcends ego and individuality, leading to a deeper connection with the divine and a greater understanding of the nature of existence.

Spiritual Courage:

Spiritual courage is the inner strength required to stay true to your beliefs and values, even when faced with challenges, doubts, or opposition. It is the resilience that allows you to continue on your spiritual path, no matter the obstacles that arise. This form of courage is not about physical bravery, but rather the steadfastness of the soul in pursuit of truth, integrity, and purpose.

Spiritual courage is rooted in a deep connection with your inner self and the conviction that your spiritual journey is worth the effort and challenges it may present. It's the ability to face the unknown, to trust in the process of growth, and to embrace the discomfort that often accompanies profound personal transformation. Spiritual courage helps you to confront fears, doubts, and societal pressures that may try to lead you away from your true path. This form of courage often involves standing up for what you believe in, even when it's unpopular or misunderstood by others. It requires the strength to express your truth, to live authentically, and to make decisions that align with your higher purpose, even when those choices are difficult or risky.

Spiritual courage involves confronting your fears rather than avoiding them. Identify specific fears or doubts that are hindering your spiritual growth and take deliberate steps to face them. Whether it's a fear of judgement, failure, or the unknown, gradually exposing yourself to these fears in manageable ways can help you build confidence and courage over time. Having a mentor or guide who embodies spiritual courage can provide you with inspiration and support. Whether it's a teacher, a spiritual leader, or a trusted friend, their guidance can help you navigate challenges with greater resilience. Regular conversations with a mentor can also offer new perspectives and strengthen your commitment to your spiritual path. Surround yourself with a community that supports your spiritual journey. Being part of a group that shares similar values and beliefs can reinforce your courage and encourage you during difficult times.

Start incorporating small acts of spiritual courage into your daily life. This could be as simple as speaking your truth in a conversation, making time for spiritual practices despite a busy schedule, or setting boundaries that honour your values. These daily practices build the habit of courage and strengthen your ability to face larger challenges. Over time, you'll be able to see your progress and recognise the strength you've developed. Writing about your experiences can also help clarify your thoughts and reinforce your commitment to your spiritual path. Engaging in acts of service and compassion can also build spiritual courage. When you focus on helping others, you often find the strength to overcome your fears and limitations. Serving others from a place of love and empathy reinforces the connection between your spiritual beliefs and actions, giving you the courage to live authentically.

Incorporate affirmations or mantras into your morning or evening routine. Spend a few minutes repeating these affirmations out loud or silently, allowing them to resonate deeply within you. This simple practice can help you stay connected to your spiritual courage throughout the day. Commit to confront one specific fear or challenge each week. It could be something small, like expressing an unpopular opinion, or something more significant, like making a life decision that aligns with your spiritual beliefs. Reflect on these experiences in your journal and note the growth in your courage over time. Set aside time each week to reflect on how you demonstrated spiritual courage. Review the challenges you faced and how you responded to them. This reflection can be done through journaling or simply in quiet contemplation. Recognising your growth reinforces your ability to continue cultivating courage.

If you have a mentor or spiritual guide, schedule regular sessions to discuss your progress and any challenges you're facing. Use these sessions as an opportunity to gain insights and encouragement, and to set new goals for your spiritual growth. Engage regularly with your spiritual community, whether it's through attending services, participating in group activities, or simply connecting with like-minded individuals. This community support strengthens your resolve and provides a network of encouragement. Make compassion a regular part of your routine. Step out of your comfort zone and build spiritual courage.

When you know that you are living in alignment with your values and beliefs, despite external challenges, you experience a profound sense of fulfilment. As you cultivate spiritual courage, your confidence grows. You become more assured in your ability to navigate life's challenges, knowing that you have the inner strength to remain true to yourself. Spiritual courage enhances your resilience, allowing you to bounce back from setbacks with greater ease. You learn to view challenges as opportunities for growth rather than as insurmountable obstacles. Spiritual courage also deepens your connections with others. When you are true to yourself, you attract relationships that are based on mutual respect and understanding.

The Practice of Meditation:

Meditation is a powerful practice that allows you to connect deeply with your inner self, bringing about a sense of peace, clarity, and balance. It is more than just a mental exercise; it's a holistic practice that impacts your mind, body, and spirit. Through meditation, you can cultivate mindfulness, enhance your emotional well-being, and develop a profound understanding of your inner world.

Meditation is the practice of focusing your mind and eliminating distractions to achieve a heightened state of awareness and inner calm. It can take many forms, from mindfulness meditation, which involves paying attention to the present moment without judgement, to concentration meditation, which involves focusing on a single point of reference like your breath, a mantra, or a candle flame. The goal of meditation is not to suppress or escape your thoughts, but to observe them with detachment, allowing you to cultivate a deeper sense of awareness and understanding.

One of the simplest and most effective meditation techniques is mindful breathing. Sit or lie down in a comfortable position, close your eyes, and bring your attention to your breath. Observe the sensation of each inhale and exhale, noticing how the air flows in and out of your body. If your mind wanders, gently bring your focus back to your breath without judgement. This practice helps anchor you in the present moment and fosters a sense of calm. This technique involves bringing awareness to different parts of your body, starting from your toes and gradually moving up to your head. As you focus on each part, notice any sensations, tension, or discomfort, and consciously relax those areas. Body scan meditation helps you develop a deeper connection with your physical self and promotes relaxation.

You repeat a word, phrase, or sound (mantra) either silently or aloud. The repetition of the mantra helps to focus the mind and reduce distractions. Common mantras include "Om,", "Peace,", or any phrase that resonates with you. The vibration of the sound and the focus on repetition can lead to a deep meditative state. Guided Visualisation, a form of meditation, involves using your imagination to create calming and peaceful images in your mind. A guide (or an audio recording) leads you through a visualisation, such as walking through a serene forest or floating on a calm ocean. Visualisation meditation can be particularly helpful for reducing stress and enhancing relaxation.

Loving-Kindness Meditation (Metta) practice involves generating feelings of love and compassion for yourself and others. Begin by focusing on yourself, silently repeating phrases like "May I be happy, may I be healthy, may I be at peace." Gradually, extend these wishes to others, including loved ones, acquaintances, and even those with whom you have conflicts. Loving-kindness meditation fosters empathy and reduces negative emotions. Walking Meditation combines the physical act of walking with mindfulness. As you walk slowly and deliberately, focus on the sensations of your feet touching the ground, the movement of your legs, and your surroundings. Walking meditation can be a refreshing alternative to seated meditation, especially for those who find it challenging to sit still for long periods.

If you're new to meditation, start with just a few minutes each day. Choose a time of day when you're least likely to be interrupted, such as early in the morning or before bed. Meditating at the same time each day helps establish a routine and makes it easier to integrate meditation into your daily life. Set a timer for your meditation sessions to prevent distractions from checking the clock. Gradually increase the time as you progress. Many meditation apps offer timers with gentle chimes to signal the end of your session. It's normal for your mind to wander during meditation. When this happens, gently bring your focus back to your chosen point of attention without judgement. Meditation doesn't have to be limited to sitting quietly. You can practice mindfulness in everyday activities like eating, washing dishes, or walking. By bringing full awareness to whatever you're doing, you can cultivate a meditative state throughout the day.

Regular meditation helps clear mental clutter and sharpens your focus. You'll find it easier to concentrate on tasks and make decisions with greater clarity. Meditation promotes emotional stability by helping you observe and process your emotions without becoming overwhelmed by them. It fosters a sense of calm and resilience, making it easier to navigate life's ups and downs.

One of the most well-known benefits of meditation is its ability to reduce stress. By calming the mind and relaxing the body, meditation helps lower stress hormones and promotes a state of relaxation. Meditation deepens your understanding of your thoughts, emotions, and behaviours. This heightened self-awareness allows you to recognise patterns and make conscious choices that align with your values. Meditation can help improve the quality of your sleep by calming the mind and reducing stress. Practices like body scan meditation or guided visualisation are particularly effective for promoting relaxation before bed. For many, meditation is a pathway to spiritual growth. It allows you to connect with your inner self and explore deeper questions about life, purpose, and existence.

The Practice of Inner Silence:

Inner silence is a profound state where the mind is free from the constant chatter of thoughts and distractions. It is not merely the absence of sound, but a deeper form that allows one to connect with their true self and the world around them. Inner silence is often considered the foundation of spiritual and mental growth, as it enables clarity, insight, and a deep sense of peace.

Inner silence is a state of consciousness where the mind becomes still, and the noise of thoughts subsides. It is not about suppressing thoughts but observing them without attachment and letting them pass without engaging. This silence is a space where the mind can rest, and true awareness can emerge. Achieving inner silence doesn't mean the absence of thoughts entirely, but rather the ability to maintain a peaceful, non-reactive state amidst them. This practice can be particularly challenging in today's world, where we are constantly bombarded with information and stimuli. However, with regular practice, it is possible to cultivate inner silence and experience its transformative benefits.

Start by becoming aware of your thoughts without judgement. When a thought arises, simply observe it and let it pass. Do not engage with it or follow it with more thoughts. This practice helps break the cycle of constant mental chatter and cultivates a state of silence. Focusing on your breath is one of the most effective ways to quiet the mind. Sit in a comfortable position and bring your attention to the natural rhythm of your breathing. As you focus on each inhale and exhale, the mind begins to calm, and thoughts start to fade into the background, allowing silence to emerge.

Dedicate time each day to sit in silence without any distractions. Find a quiet place where you won't be disturbed. Sit comfortably, close your eyes, and allow yourself to be present in the silence. This practice helps you become comfortable with stillness and trains the mind to find peace in quiet moments. Use a simple mantra like "silence" or "peace" to focus your mind. Repeat the word silently in your mind, allowing it to anchor your thoughts and bring you back to a state of calm whenever your mind starts to wander. Spending time in nature can naturally cultivate inner silence. The serene environment, free from artificial noise, allows your mind to settle into a peaceful rhythm. Whether it's a walk in the forest, sitting by a river, or simply being in a quiet park, nature has a way of quieting the mind and fostering inner silence.

Upon waking, instead of reaching for your phone or getting caught up in the day's tasks, sit quietly and breathe. This practice sets a peaceful tone for the day and helps you maintain a calm mind. Throughout the day, take short breaks dedicated to silence. These breaks don't have to be long, just a few minutes of sitting quietly or focusing on your breath can reset your mind and bring you back to a state of calm. End your day with silence. Before going to bed, sit quietly and reflect on your day without judgement. Allow any thoughts or emotions to pass through your mind without clinging to them. This practice helps in let go of the day's stresses and prepares you for a restful sleep. Dedicate time each day when you disconnect from technology. Turn off your phone, computer, and other devices, and allow yourself to be present in the silence. This practice helps reduce mental noise and fosters a deeper connection with your inner self. Engage in activities that naturally promote silence, such as yoga, tai chi, or mindful walking. These practices combine movement with awareness and encourage a state of inner peace and calm.

Inner silence clears away mental clutter, allowing you to think more clearly and make decisions with greater insight. It creates space for new ideas and perspectives to emerge. When the mind is quiet, emotions are less likely to overwhelm you. Inner silence helps you observe your emotions without being controlled by them, leading to greater emotional balance. Silence sharpens your awareness, both of your inner world and the world around you. It also enhances your ability to notice subtleties, whether in your thoughts, emotions, or environment. For many, inner silence is a pathway to deeper spiritual connection. It allows you to tune into your inner self and the larger universe, fostering a sense of oneness and peace. Inner silence is a powerful antidote to stress. A quiet mind is often more creative. When the constant chatter subsides, new ideas, solutions, and inspirations can arise naturally.

Living in the Present Moment:

Living in the present moment is a profound practice that focuses on fully experiencing and engaging with the current time rather than being preoccupied with the past or future. This concept, often referred to as mindfulness or present-moment awareness, is a cornerstone of many spiritual and psychological practices. By anchoring yourself in the present, you can enhance your overall well-being, reduce stress, and cultivate a richer, more fulfilling life.

The present moment is the immediate experience of now. It is the space where life unfolds and where you have the most direct access to your thoughts, feelings, and surroundings. Unlike the past, which is a series of memories, and the future, which is a realm of anticipation, the present moment is real and tangible. It is where your life is happening. Living in the present moment requires shifting your focus from dwelling on what has already happened or what might happen. It involves recognising that the only time you can truly control and experience is the current moment. This shift can lead to greater clarity, reduced anxiety, and a deeper connection with yourself and others.

Engage your senses to fully experience the present. Notice the colours, textures, sounds, and smells around you. By consciously observing your environment through your senses, you ground yourself in the here and now. This practice involves mentally scanning your body from head to toe, observing any sensations, tensions, or areas of discomfort. It helps you connect with your physical presence and encourages awareness of the current state of your body. Focus on one task at a time rather than multitasking. Give your full attention to whatever you are doing, whether it's eating, working, or engaging in a conversation. This practice enhances your ability to be present and reduces distractions.

When interacting with others, practice active listening without planning your response or letting your mind wander. Fully engage with the speaker, paying attention to their words, tone, and body language. This fosters deeper connections and keeps you grounded in the moment. Assess moments where you were fully present and areas where you were distracted. This practice helps you become more aware of your habits and encourages a more mindful approach to living.

Approach meals with mindfulness. Pay attention to the colours, textures, and flavours of your food. Chew slowly and savour each bite. This practice enhances your enjoyment of food and helps you remain present during mealtimes. Incorporate mindfulness into physical activities such as walking, exercising, or even cleaning. Focus on the sensations of movement, your body's response, and the environment around you. This turns routine tasks into opportunities for presence. Allocate specific times to disconnect from digital devices. Use this time to engage in activities that foster presence, such as reading a book, spending time with loved ones, or enjoying nature. Review the day's events with a focus on moments where you were present and areas where you can improve. This practice helps you learn from your experiences and enhances your ability to stay grounded in the present.

By focusing on the present, you can avoid the anxiety that comes from worrying about the future or dwelling on past mistakes. This reduces overall stress and fosters a sense of calm. Present-moment awareness improves your ability to concentrate and be productive. When you are fully engaged with the task at hand, you work more efficiently and with greater effectiveness. Being present in conversations and interactions strengthens your connections with others. It shows that you value and respect their presence, leading to more meaningful and fulfilling relationships. When you are fully immersed in the present, you experience life more vividly. This helps you appreciate the beauty and richness of life.

Living in the present moment helps you respond to challenges with greater emotional stability. You are less likely to be overwhelmed by negative emotions and more able to handle difficulties with a balanced perspective. Present-moment awareness fosters a deeper understanding of your thoughts, feelings, and behaviours. This self-awareness leads to personal growth and a more authentic connection with yourself.

The Power of Prayer:

Prayer is a profound spiritual practice found in many religious and spiritual traditions. It involves communicating with a higher power, the divine, or the universe, seeking guidance, expressing gratitude, and finding solace. While prayer practices vary widely, the underlying principle remains consistent: prayer connects individuals to a greater force and can profoundly impact their mental, emotional, and spiritual well-being. Understanding and harnessing the power of prayer can lead to a more meaningful and fulfilling life.

Prayer is not merely a ritual but a dynamic practice that fosters a deeper connection with one's inner self and the divine. It serves as a channel for expressing desires, concerns, and gratitude. Through prayer, individuals seek to align their intentions with a higher purpose and draw upon spiritual strength. The act of praying can be transformative, influencing one's outlook on life and enhancing overall well-being.

Begin each prayer with a clear intention. Whether seeking guidance, expressing gratitude, or asking for support, defining your purpose helps focus your mind and heart. Intentional prayer ensures that your communication is purposeful and aligned with your spiritual needs. Designate a quiet, peaceful space for prayer. A sacred space enhances the experience of prayer by providing an environment free from distractions and conducive to spiritual reflection. Frame your prayers positively and affirmatively. Instead of focusing on what you lack or fear, express your desires and intentions with confidence. Affirmative language aligns with the principle of attracting positive energy and reinforces your faith in the outcome.

Combine prayer with meditation to deepen your spiritual practice. After reciting your prayer, spend a few moments in silence, focusing on your breath and the sense of connection with the divine. Meditation enhances your ability to receive guidance and insights from your prayers. Begin and end your prayer with expressions of gratitude. Acknowledging the blessings in your life shifts your focus from what you lack to what you have.

Keep a prayer journal to document your prayers, thoughts, and any insights you receive. Writing down your prayers provides clarity and helps track your spiritual growth over time. It also allows you to reflect on the answers and guidance received. Participate in group prayer or spiritual gatherings to enhance your practice. Sharing prayer with others fosters a sense of community and collective energy. Group prayer amplifies the power of individual intentions and supports shared spiritual goals.

Include prayer in your daily routine by starting and ending your day with a moment of reflection. Morning prayers set a positive tone for the day, while evening prayers offer an opportunity for gratitude and contemplation. Take short prayer breaks throughout your day. These moments of pause provide an opportunity to reconnect with your spiritual intentions and find solace amidst daily activities. Use these breaks to centre yourself and realign with your higher purpose. Turn to prayer during significant life events or challenges. Whether facing a major decision, experiencing difficulty, or celebrating a milestone, prayer offers guidance, strength, and support. Embrace prayer as a tool for navigating both joyous and challenging times. Extend your prayers to others in need.

The act of praying can alleviate anxiety and promote a sense of inner peace. Regular prayer cultivates mental clarity and focus. By aligning your intentions with a higher purpose, prayer helps you navigate challenges with a clear and centred mind. It supports decision-making and reinforces your spiritual goals. Prayer reinforces your faith and spiritual resilience. By connecting with the divine and seeking guidance, you build a sense of trust in the universe's plan. This faith strengthens your ability to cope with difficulties and persevere through life's challenges.

Engaging in prayer fosters a sense of connection with the divine and with others who share similar beliefs. This connection provides a sense of belonging and support, enhancing your spiritual journey and overall well-being. Offering prayers for others cultivates compassion and empathy. It encourages a broader perspective and deepens your understanding of others' experiences. Prayer fosters a sense of unity and collective support within the community.

Rising Above Desires:

Desires are intrinsic to the human experience, influencing our choices and behaviours. While desires can drive ambition and personal growth, unchecked or unbalanced desires can lead to stress, dissatisfaction, and a sense of emptiness. Rising above desires involves cultivating inner freedom and finding contentment beyond material or fleeting wants. This practice is essential for spiritual growth and achieving lasting peace.

Desires are natural and reflect our aspirations and needs. They range from basic necessities like food and shelter to more complex yearnings for status, pleasure, or success. However, when desires become overwhelming or define our sense of self-worth, they can create a cycle of craving and dissatisfaction. Rising above desires means recognising and managing these urges without allowing them to dominate your life.

The first step in rising above desires is developing self-awareness. Observe your desires without judgement and understand their origins and impact on your life. Journaling your thoughts and feelings can help clarify which desires are aligned with your true values and which may be leading you astray. Engage in mindful reflection to gain insight into the nature of your desires. Ask yourself why you want something and whether it aligns with your deeper goals and values. Identify what truly matters to you, such as relationships, personal growth, or contribution to society, and focus on these values. By prioritising values over desires, you create a more meaningful and fulfilling life.

Practice detachment from material possessions and transient experiences. Detachment involves recognising that external achievements and possessions do not define your worth or happiness. By letting go of attachment to specific outcomes, you foster a sense of inner freedom and resilience. Simplify your life by reducing unnecessary distractions and focusing on essential activities. A minimalist approach to living can help you prioritise what truly matters and diminish the influence of superficial desires. Simplification creates space for deeper connections and personal growth.

Develop self-discipline to manage desires and impulses. Self-discipline involves making conscious choices that align with your long-term goals and values, even when faced with immediate temptations. Techniques such as delayed gratification and setting boundaries can enhance your ability to rise above desires.

Before making a purchase or engaging in an activity, pause to consider whether it aligns with your values and contributes to your well-being. Mindful consumption helps prevent impulsive decisions driven by desires. Structure your daily routine to include activities that nourish your mind, body, and spirit. By focusing on meaningful and fulfilling activities, you reduce the influence of transient desires and create a balanced and purposeful life. Surround yourself with supportive individuals who share your values and goals. Engage in conversations and activities that reinforce your commitment to rising above desires. A supportive community can provide encouragement and accountability. Approach yourself with self-compassion when dealing with desires. Recognise that it is normal to experience desires and that rising above them is a gradual process. Be patient with yourself and acknowledge your progress along the way.

Rising above desires leads to greater inner peace and contentment. By focusing on values and long-term goals, you reduce the stress and anxiety associated with unfulfilled desires. The practice of rising above desires fosters self-awareness and personal growth. Understanding your motivations and aligning them with your values leads to a more authentic and fulfilling life. Developing the ability to manage desires enhances your resilience in the face of challenges. You become less dependent on external validation and more capable of navigating life's ups and downs with equanimity. By prioritising values and meaningful goals over transient desires, you experience deeper fulfilment and satisfaction. This fulfilment comes from living in alignment with your true self and contributing to a greater purpose.

Understanding Maya:

In many spiritual and philosophical traditions, Maya is a term that signifies the illusionary nature of the material world. Derived from Sanskrit, Maya often translates to "illusion" or "deception," reflecting the idea that the physical world we perceive is not the ultimate reality but rather a transient and deceptive appearance. Understanding Maya involves exploring the nature of this illusion and how it impacts our perception of reality. Maya refers to the veil that obscures our perception of the true nature of existence. According to various Eastern philosophies, including Hinduism and Buddhism, Maya is responsible for creating the illusion of separateness and materiality. It is through Maya that the finite and impermanent nature of the physical world appears to be real, masking the underlying unity and eternal essence.

Engage in philosophical inquiry to explore the nature of reality and illusion. Study ancient texts and teachings that discuss Maya, such as the Upanishads, Bhagavad Gita, or Buddhist sutras. Reflect on the concepts of impermanence, suffering, and the true self to gain a deeper understanding of Maya. Meditation is a powerful tool for transcending the illusion of Maya. Practice mindfulness and contemplative meditation to observe your thoughts, emotions, and perceptions. Through meditation, you can gain insights into the nature of your mind and how it contributes to the illusion of reality. Conduct self-inquiry to explore the nature of your own identity and beliefs. Question the assumptions you hold about yourself and the world around you. By examining the sense of ego and personal identity, you can begin to uncover the illusory aspects of your perception.

Contemplate the impermanent nature of all phenomena. Recognise that everything in the physical world – objects, experiences, and even emotions – is subject to change and decay. By acknowledging impermanence, you can see through the illusion of permanence and stability that Maya creates. Dive into sacred texts and teachings that address the concept of Maya. Texts such as the Vedas, Bhagavad Gita, or Buddhist scriptures provide insights into the nature of illusion and the path to transcendence. Study these texts with an open mind and seek guidance from knowledgeable teachers.

Cultivate detachment from material possessions, desires, and outcomes. Recognise that attachment to transient things reinforces the illusion of separateness and permanence. By practising detachment, you can begin to see beyond the surface appearance of reality. Engage in practices that facilitate experiences of transcendence, such as deep meditation, spiritual retreats, or mystical experiences. These experiences can provide direct insights into the nature of reality and the illusion of Maya, helping you to perceive beyond the ordinary.

Apply the insights gained from understanding Maya to your daily life by living mindfully. Recognise the transient nature of your experiences and interactions. Approach life with a sense of openness and acceptance, knowing that all phenomena are temporary. Embrace simplicity and minimalism as a way to counteract the distractions and attachments created by Maya. By focusing on essential needs and reducing clutter, you can cultivate a clearer perspective on what truly matters. Make time for regular reflection on the nature of reality and illusion. Set aside moments for contemplation and meditation to deepen your understanding of Maya. Use these reflections to guide your actions and decisions.

Seek wisdom from spiritual teachers, mentors, or communities that explore the nature of Maya. Engage in discussions and practices that challenge your perceptions and expand your understanding of reality. Develop inner awareness through practices such as journaling, self-reflection, and mindful observation. By increasing your awareness of your thoughts and emotions, you can gain insights into how Maya influences your perception of reality.

Understanding Maya brings clarity to your perception of reality. By recognising the illusory aspects of the material world, you can see beyond superficial appearances and grasp a deeper sense of truth. Gaining insight into Maya can lead to greater freedom from attachment and suffering. By seeing through the illusion of permanence and separateness, you can experience a sense of liberation and inner peace. Understanding the nature of Maya fosters a deeper connection with the underlying unity of existence. It allows you to transcend individual ego and experience a sense of oneness with the world and others.

With an understanding of Maya, you develop a more balanced perspective on life. You become less affected by temporary challenges and distractions, focusing instead on what truly matters. Exploring Maya contributes to your spiritual growth by deepening your understanding of the nature of reality and the self.

The Role of Guru:

In many spiritual traditions, the concept of the "Guru" (a Sanskrit term meaning "teacher" or "guide") holds a central place. The Guru is regarded as a source of wisdom, guidance, and spiritual awakening. The Rule of Guru refers to the principles and practices associated with seeking, respecting, and learning from a spiritual teacher. Understanding and following the Rule of the Guru involves recognising the role of the teacher in your spiritual journey and integrating their guidance into your life. The Guru serves as a bridge between the seeker and the ultimate truth. They provide insights, teachings, and practices that help individuals navigate the complexities of spiritual growth. The Guru's role is not merely to impart knowledge but to inspire and transform the disciple through personal example and guidance. The Guru helps the seeker understand deeper truths and overcome obstacles on the path to enlightenment.

The first principle of the Role of the Guru is to show deep respect and reverence for the Guru. This respect is not just a formality, but a recognition of the Guru's role in your spiritual journey. Reverence creates a space for learning and transformation, allowing the teachings to penetrate your consciousness. Approach the Guru with an open mind and a willingness to learn. The Guru may challenge your existing beliefs and push you out of your comfort zone. Being open to new perspectives and practices is crucial for effective guidance and personal growth.

Dedicate yourself to learning from the Guru. This involves consistent study of their teachings, participation in their practices, and application of their guidance in daily life. The commitment to learning fosters a deeper connection with the Guru and accelerates your spiritual progress. Trust the Guru's guidance and the process of spiritual development. There may be times when you feel uncertain or face difficulties, but maintaining faith in the Guru's wisdom and the path they have laid out is essential for overcoming challenges and achieving growth. Follow the practices and disciplines recommended by the Guru. The Guru provides a framework for spiritual practice, and adhering to these guidelines requires self-discipline.

Engage in regular study of the Guru's teachings. This can include reading their books, listening to their lectures, and reflecting on their wisdom. Regular study keeps you aligned with the Guru's guidance and deepens your understanding of spiritual principles. Implement the practices recommended by the Guru in your daily life. This may include meditation, prayer, ethical conduct, or other spiritual disciplines. Applying these practices helps you internalise the teachings and experience their transformative effects.

When possible, seek personal guidance from the Guru. This could involve one-on-one meetings, consultations, or spiritual counselling. Personal guidance provides tailored advice and support for specific challenges you may be facing. Cultivate a devotional attitude towards the Guru. This involves expressing gratitude, participating in devotional practices, and honouring the Guru's teachings through your actions. Devotion enhances your connection with the Guru and aligns your heart with spiritual goals. Engage with a community of fellow seekers who are also following the Guru's teachings. Being part of a supportive community provides encouragement, shared experiences, and collective wisdom. It also helps you stay motivated and committed to your spiritual path.

The Guru's wisdom and experience help you navigate the complexities of spiritual growth, making the journey more effective and rewarding. The Guru's teachings offer clarity on spiritual principles and practices. This clarity helps you understand your path, make informed decisions, and avoid common pitfalls. The guidance of a Guru fosters personal transformation. Through their teachings and example, you can overcome inner obstacles, develop virtues, and achieve greater spiritual realisation. This deeper understanding enriches your spiritual practice and enhances your overall sense of fulfilment and purpose. The Guru provides supportive guidance during challenging times. Their experience and compassion offer reassurance and practical advice, helping you navigate difficulties.

Include regular study of the Guru's teachings and daily practice of their recommended disciplines into your routine. Consistency in these areas helps you stay connected with the Guru's guidance and supports ongoing growth. Regularly express devotion towards the Guru. This can be through prayer, offerings, or acts of service. Expressing gratitude reinforces your connection with the Guru and acknowledges their role in your spiritual journey. Whenever possible, seek opportunities for personal interaction with the Guru or their representatives. Personal interactions provide valuable insights and support tailored to your individual needs. Engage with a community of like-minded individuals who follow the Guru's teachings. Participate in group activities, discussions, and spiritual practices to strengthen your commitment and benefit from shared experiences.

The Power of Devotion:

Devotion, often described as a profound and unwavering commitment to a higher power or principle, plays a crucial role in spiritual and personal growth. It involves a deep emotional and spiritual attachment, guiding actions and thoughts towards the divine or a higher purpose. The power of devotion transcends mere belief or routine; it fosters a transformative connection that can significantly influence one's life path and inner experience.

Devotion is more than just religious or spiritual practice; it's an expression of love, faith, and dedication towards something greater than oneself. It manifests as a sincere commitment that often leads to profound personal transformation. In spiritual contexts, devotion is directed towards a deity, a spiritual teacher, or the universal principles of existence. Genuine devotion arises from a place of authenticity and sincerity. It requires a true alignment of heart and mind, where actions reflect deep-seated beliefs and emotions. Authentic devotion is not performed for show or external approval but stems from a profound inner conviction. True devotion often involves sacrifice and selflessness.

Devotion is deeply intertwined with love and compassion. It involves nurturing a loving relationship with the divine, oneself, or others, which in turn encourages acts of kindness, understanding, and empathy. Inspiration helps maintain motivation and deepens your connection. Devotion strengthens your connection to spiritual beliefs or practices, leading to a deeper sense of purpose and fulfilment. It nurtures a deep-seated sense of contentment and joy that arises from living in alignment with your highest values and aspirations.

Include devotional practices in your daily routine. Consistency in practices such as meditation, prayer, or reflection helps reinforce your commitment and creates a stable foundation for spiritual growth. Participate in communities or groups that share your devotional interests. Engaging with like-minded individuals provides support, encouragement, and shared experiences that enrich your practice.

Recognise and celebrate milestones in your devotional journey. Acknowledge progress, achievements, and moments of insight to maintain motivation and deepen your connection. Allow your practice of devotion to evolve as you grow. Be open to adapting your practices, beliefs, or rituals to reflect changes in your understanding and experiences. Regularly reflect on your devotional journey and renew your commitment. Re-evaluate your practices, intentions, and goals to ensure they align with your evolving understanding and aspirations.

The Importance of Truth:

Truth is often heralded as a fundamental value in personal and collective growth. It represents the pursuit of honesty, clarity, and integrity, and acts as a guiding principle for making decisions and forming relationships. Embracing the importance of truth fosters authenticity, builds trust, and paves the way for meaningful progress and self-improvement. Truth is not merely the alignment of words with facts but encompasses a deeper alignment with reality, principles, and personal values. Truth is an essential component of personal integrity, where one's actions and beliefs are consistent with their understanding of reality.

At its core, truth involves honesty, where one's statements and actions are genuine and transparent. Honesty is crucial for establishing trust and credibility in relationships and interactions. It requires a commitment to presenting oneself and one's intentions clearly and accurately. Integrity reflects a consistent adherence to truth, even when faced with challenges or temptations. Understanding and accepting one's truths requires self-awareness. This involves recognising personal biases, limitations, and motivations. Self-awareness helps in identifying and addressing discrepancies between one's values and behaviours, fostering personal growth and authenticity.

Transparency involves openly sharing information and intentions. It creates an environment of openness and trust, where individuals feel secure in their interactions and communications. Transparency is vital for fostering collaborative and honest relationships. Embracing truth also means taking responsibility for one's actions and decisions. Accountability involves acknowledging mistakes, learning from them, and making amends when necessary. It reflects a commitment to personal growth and ethical conduct.

Focus on expressing yourself clearly and listening actively to others. Mindful communication encourages authenticity and reduces misunderstandings. Actively seek feedback from trusted individuals to gain an external perspective on your actions and behaviour. Develop empathy to understand and appreciate different perspectives and truths. Empathy involves seeing situations from others' viewpoints and acknowledging their experiences. Avoid conforming to external expectations or pretending to be someone you're not. Authenticity reinforces personal integrity and builds genuine connections with others. Embrace mistakes as opportunities for growth and learning. Acknowledge errors, take responsibility, and make necessary adjustments to align more closely with your understanding of truth.

Summary:

In this chapter, we learned about key aspects of spiritual growth and self-realisation. We explored the nature of the soul and the deeper purpose of life. The chapter emphasised the power of faith and the idea that all beings are interconnected. It highlighted the importance of spiritual courage and overcoming challenges and discussed practices like meditation, prayer, and inner silence for deepening our connection with ourselves.

We also learned about living in the present moment to achieve mindfulness and peace, and how rising above desires and understanding

"Maya" (illusion) is important for spiritual freedom. The chapter covered the role of the Guru in guiding us, the impact of devotion, and the significance of truth and persistence on our spiritual journey. It served as a guide for finding deeper meaning and a closer connection to our spiritual selves.

Chapter 6 – Knowledge and Devotion

Source: saatchiart.com

> *"Bhakti is not destructive; it teaches that all our faculties may become means to reach salvation. We must turn them all towards God and give to Him that love which is usually wasted on the fleeting objects of sense."*
>
> *–Swami Vivekananda*

Bhakti (devotion) is a positive force, not something harmful. It shows that all our abilities and emotions can help us reach a higher spiritual understanding or salvation. Instead of focusing on temporary pleasures and worldly things, we should direct our love and energy towards God or a higher purpose. By doing this, we transform our devotion into a way of gaining deeper knowledge and spiritual growth, using our emotions and thoughts to connect with the divine.

The Balance of Knowledge and Devotion:

Balancing knowledge and devotion is essential for a well-rounded spiritual and intellectual life. While knowledge represents our intellectual pursuits, understanding, and the pursuit of truth, devotion embodies our emotional connection, faith, and spiritual commitment. Achieving equilibrium between these two aspects fosters holistic growth, ensuring that our intellectual capabilities are harmonised with our spiritual aspirations. This balance is important for personal development and attaining a deeper understanding of oneself and the universe. Balancing knowledge and devotion involves integrating intellectual exploration with spiritual practices. Each aspect complements the other, contributing to a richer and more fulfilling life.

Knowledge involves the acquisition of information, critical thinking, and intellectual understanding. It empowers us with the ability to analyse, reason, and solve problems. Knowledge also deepens our understanding of the world and our place in it. Devotion represents emotional and spiritual commitment, faith, and the practice of spiritual disciplines. Devotion connects us to our inner self, the divine, and the values that guide our lives. It nurtures our emotional well-being and spiritual growth.

Combine intellectual study with spiritual practices. For instance, while studying philosophical texts or scientific principles, incorporate meditation or prayer to reflect on how these concepts align with your spiritual beliefs. This integration helps in bridging the gap between intellect and spirituality. Define clear objectives for both your intellectual and spiritual pursuits. Having distinct goals for each area allows you to allocate time and effort appropriately. Ensure that these objectives complement each other and contribute to your overall growth. Allocate specific times for intellectual and spiritual activities. For example, you might designate certain hours for studying and other times for meditation or devotional practices. Having a structured schedule helps in maintaining balance and ensuring that both areas receive attention.

Engage in regular reflection to assess how your intellectual pursuits and spiritual practices are influencing each other. Reflect on questions such as: How does your knowledge enhance your spiritual understanding? How does your devotion impact your intellectual curiosity? Reflection helps in aligning your efforts and making necessary adjustments. Look for opportunities where knowledge and devotion intersect. For example, studying sacred texts from various traditions can offer insights into spiritual practices, while devotional practices can inspire intellectual curiosity. Seek out learning experiences that enrich both your mind and spirit. Adopt a holistic approach to personal development that values both intellectual and spiritual growth. Recognise that true wisdom encompasses both understanding and experience. Balance your intellectual achievements with spiritual growth to achieve a harmonious and fulfilling life.

Explore interdisciplinary studies that merge intellectual inquiry with spiritual exploration. For instance, studying the philosophy of religion, ethics, or spiritual psychology can provide insights into the relationship between knowledge and devotion. Practice mindful reading of both intellectual and spiritual texts. As you read, reflect on how the content resonates with your own beliefs and experiences. Use this practice to deepen your understanding and enhance your spiritual connection.

Participate in discussions and debates with others who share similar interests. Engaging in conversations about intellectual and spiritual topics can provide new perspectives and insights, fostering a balanced approach to learning and devotion. Attend workshops, seminars, or retreats that focus on integrating knowledge and devotion. These events often offer opportunities to learn from experts and practitioners who emphasise the importance of balancing intellectual and spiritual growth. Practice mindfulness in both intellectual and devotional activities. Mindfulness enhances your awareness and focus, allowing you to engage more deeply in both study and spiritual practices.

Balancing knowledge and devotion leads to a deeper understanding of both intellectual concepts and spiritual truths. It fosters holistic personal growth, integrating intellectual, emotional, and spiritual aspects of life. The synergy between knowledge and devotion cultivates wisdom, providing a more comprehensive perspective on life and its challenges. Achieving a balance between knowledge and devotion contributes to a sense of fulfilment and purpose, aligning your intellectual pursuits with your spiritual values. Harmonising these aspects supports overall well-being, enhancing both mental clarity and emotional resilience.

Develop a routine that includes time for both intellectual activities and spiritual practices. Ensure that each aspect receives attention and that your routine reflects your commitment to balanced growth. Embrace a mindset of continuous learning and growth. Stay open to new ideas and experiences that enrich both your intellectual and spiritual life, fostering a dynamic and balanced approach.

The Journey from Knowledge to Wisdom:

The journey from knowledge to wisdom is a profound and transformative process. Knowledge represents the accumulation of facts, information, and understanding acquired through study and experience. Wisdom, on the other hand, is the application of that knowledge in a meaningful and insightful way, incorporating deeper understanding, discernment, and compassion. This journey involves not just acquiring information but evolving through experiences, reflections, and personal growth. This guide explores the stages and practices involved in making this transition from knowledge to wisdom.

Acquisition of Knowledge is the initial stage involving gathering information and developing understanding through various means such as education, reading, and observation. This stage is characterised by the accumulation of facts, concepts, and theoretical insights. It lays the groundwork for deeper exploration. As knowledge is acquired, the next step is to integrate it into one's understanding and reflect on its implications. This involves connecting new information with existing knowledge, analysing its relevance, and contemplating its broader significance. Reflection helps in consolidating knowledge and preparing for the application of wisdom. Knowledge becomes wisdom when it is applied in real-life situations. This stage involves using acquired knowledge to make decisions, solve problems, and navigate challenges. Experience plays a crucial role here, as the practical application provides deeper insights and helps refine one's understanding.

Through application and reflection, individuals begin to develop insight. This is characterised by an enhanced ability to see patterns, make connections, and understand underlying principles. Insight represents a deeper level of understanding that goes beyond superficial knowledge. Wisdom also involves discernment, the ability to judge and make decisions based on a combination of knowledge, insight, and ethical considerations. This stage focuses on developing the capacity to weigh different factors, consider long-term consequences, and make balanced decisions.

True wisdom encompasses compassion and empathy, recognising the interconnectedness of all beings and the impact of one's actions on others. This stage involves applying knowledge and insight with a sense of empathy and ethical responsibility. The journey from knowledge to wisdom is continuous. It requires ongoing growth, adaptation, and openness to new experiences and perspectives. Lifelong learning and self-awareness are essential for maintaining and deepening wisdom over time.

Regularly set aside time for deep reflection on your experiences, decisions, and the knowledge you have acquired. Use journaling or meditation to explore how your knowledge can be applied and what insights you can gain from it. Expand your understanding by seeking diverse perspectives and engaging in conversations with others who have different experiences and viewpoints. This helps in broadening your horizon and enhancing your discernment. When applying knowledge, practice mindfulness to ensure that your decisions and actions are guided by wisdom. Consider the ethical implications and potential impact on others. Embrace experiences as opportunities for growth. Reflect on both successes and failures to gain insights and refine your understanding. Experience is a powerful teacher that deepens knowledge and fosters wisdom.

Develop emotional intelligence by understanding and managing your emotions and empathising with others. Emotional intelligence enhances your ability to apply knowledge wisely and compassionately. Maintain a commitment to lifelong learning and personal development. Stay curious, seek new knowledge, and remain open to evolving your understanding. This ongoing process supports the continual growth of wisdom. Find mentors or guides who can provide wisdom and insights based on their experiences. Learning from others who have navigated the journey from knowledge to wisdom can offer valuable guidance and support.

Reflect on how your knowledge applies to your life and the broader context. Develop a framework for ethical decision-making that considers the long-term consequences and the well-being of others. Apply this framework to your decisions and actions to align with wisdom. Practice empathetic listening in your interactions with others. Understand their perspectives and experiences, and use this understanding to inform your decisions and actions. Cultivate gratitude for the knowledge and experiences you have gained. Embrace humility, recognising that wisdom is a journey with no final destination and that there is always more to learn. Align your knowledge and actions with your core values and principles. Ensure that your pursuit of wisdom reflects a commitment to living authentically and ethically.

Wisdom improves decision-making by incorporating insight, discernment, and ethical considerations. It helps in making more balanced and thoughtful choices. The transition from knowledge to wisdom provides a deeper and more nuanced understanding of life, relationships, and the world. Wisdom fosters compassion and empathy, enhancing your ability to connect with others and contribute positively to their lives. Achieving wisdom leads to a sense of fulfilment and purpose, as it integrates intellectual growth with emotional and ethical development. The journey from knowledge to wisdom supports ongoing personal and spiritual growth, fostering a lifelong pursuit of learning and self-improvement.

Practical Applications of Knowledge:

The practical application of knowledge involves translating theoretical understanding into actionable steps and real-world solutions. It is the bridge between knowing and doing, where abstract concepts are tested, refined, and utilised to address real-life challenges and opportunities. Effective application of knowledge not only demonstrates its relevance but also contributes to personal growth, innovation, and problem-solving. This guide explores how to apply knowledge practically, offering techniques and practices to ensure that theoretical insights lead to tangible outcomes. Practical application is the process of implementing knowledge to achieve specific goals or solve problems.

Applying knowledge effectively requires understanding the context in which it will be used. This involves recognising the specific needs, constraints, and opportunities within a given situation. Before applying knowledge, it is essential to identify the problems or challenges that need to be addressed. Clear problem identification ensures that the application is targeted and relevant. Based on the identified problem, design solutions that leverage the knowledge acquired. This involves creating actionable plans, strategies, or interventions that address the problem effectively. Execute the designed solutions in a practical setting. This phase involves putting plans into action, monitoring progress, and making necessary adjustments. After implementation, evaluate the effectiveness of the applied knowledge. Collect feedback, assess outcomes, and reflect on the success and areas for improvement.

Set specific, measurable, achievable, relevant, and time-bound (SMART) objectives for applying knowledge. Clear objectives provide direction and focus, ensuring that the application is purposeful and aligned with desired outcomes. Create detailed action plans outlining the steps required to implement knowledge effectively. Include timelines, resources, and responsibilities to guide the application process. Apply knowledge to real-world scenarios or case studies to test its practicality and relevance. This approach helps in understanding how theoretical concepts work in different contexts and enhances problem-solving skills.

Utilise technology and tools that can support the application of knowledge. For example, software applications, data analytics, and digital platforms can enhance efficiency and effectiveness in implementing solutions. Engage with experts or mentors who can provide insights and guidance on applying knowledge. Collaboration can offer valuable perspectives and enhance the quality of practical applications. Before full-scale implementation, conduct pilot tests or trials to evaluate the feasibility and effectiveness of the applied knowledge. Pilot testing allows for adjustments and refinements based on real-world feedback. Continuously monitor the implementation process and make necessary adjustments based on feedback and performance. Flexibility and adaptability are crucial for optimising the application of knowledge.

Seek opportunities for hands-on experience where you can directly apply knowledge. This could involve internships, projects, or practical exercises that allow you to test and refine your understanding in a real-world setting. Focus on solving real problems or addressing challenges within your area of expertise. Applying knowledge to meaningful issues ensures that your efforts have a tangible impact and contribute to practical outcomes. After applying knowledge, take time to reflect on the experience. Analyse what worked well, what could be improved, and how the application of knowledge can be enhanced in future endeavours.

Share your findings and applications with others in your field. Collaborating and exchanging ideas can lead to new insights, improvements, and innovative solutions. Keep abreast of new developments and advancements in your field. Staying updated ensures that your application of knowledge remains relevant and incorporates the latest insights and practices. Document the processes, outcomes, and lessons learned from applying knowledge. Regularly review and update the documentation to reflect new experiences and improvements. Embrace a growth mindset by viewing challenges and failures as opportunities for learning and development. This mindset encourages continuous improvement and adaptability in applying knowledge.

Applying knowledge practically improves problem-solving skills by providing real-world challenges and opportunities for creative solutions. Practical application demonstrates the relevance and utility of knowledge, ensuring that theoretical insights contribute to tangible outcomes and impact. Engaging in practical applications fosters personal growth by expanding skills, enhancing expertise, and building confidence in one's abilities. The application of knowledge often leads to innovative solutions and improvements in processes, products, or services. Practical application has the potential to make a significant impact on individuals, organisations, and communities by addressing real needs and challenges.

How to Apply Spiritual and Philosophical Knowledge in Daily Life:

Applying spiritual and philosophical knowledge in daily life involves integrating timeless wisdom and ethical principles into everyday actions, decisions, and interactions. This practice enriches personal growth, fosters inner peace, and enhances relationships. The integration of such knowledge transforms abstract concepts into practical behaviours that align with one's values and aspirations. This guide outlines how to seamlessly incorporate spiritual and philosophical insights into daily routines, enhancing both personal and communal well-being.

Spiritual and philosophical knowledge often encompasses principles such as mindfulness, compassion, ethics, and self-awareness. It provides guidance in understanding the nature of existence, the meaning of life, and the cultivation of virtues.

Use philosophical principles to guide your decision-making process. For example, apply the ethical principle of utilitarianism (maximising overall happiness) or virtue ethics (focusing on character and virtues) to evaluate choices and actions. Practice compassion and empathy in your interactions with others. The teachings of many spiritual and philosophical traditions emphasise the importance of kindness and understanding in building meaningful relationships. Align your daily activities with your spiritual and philosophical values. This might involve setting goals that reflect your beliefs, choosing work or hobbies that resonate with your sense of purpose, or engaging in acts of service to support others.

Include spiritual rituals or symbols in your daily life as reminders of your values and beliefs. This could include lighting a candle for meditation, carrying a meaningful object, or practising daily affirmations. Cultivate a practice of gratitude by acknowledging and appreciating the positive aspects of your life. Reflect on what you are grateful for and how these aspects align with your spiritual or philosophical understanding. Engage with community and service opportunities that reflect your spiritual or philosophical values. Volunteering or participating in community activities can provide a sense of connection and purpose. Commit to ongoing study and learning about spiritual and philosophical teachings. Reading books, attending lectures, or participating in discussions can deepen your understanding and application of these insights.

Set goals and make plans that reflect your spiritual or philosophical values. For example, if you value compassion, set goals related to helping others or contributing to social causes. Conclude your day with a reflection on how your actions and experiences aligned with your spiritual or philosophical principles. Consider what went well and areas for improvement. Include small acts of kindness in your daily routine. Whether it's a kind word, a helping hand, or a supportive gesture, these actions embody the principles of compassion and love. Strive for balance in your life by integrating spiritual and philosophical insights into various aspects, such as work, relationships, and personal growth. Avoid extremes and seek harmony in your pursuits.

Integrating spiritual and philosophical knowledge into daily life promotes emotional and psychological well-being, and provides a sense of purpose and inner peace. Applying principles of compassion, empathy, and ethical behaviour fosters healthier and more meaningful relationships with others. Spiritual and philosophical teachings offer perspectives that enhance resilience, helping you navigate life's challenges with grace and confidence. Aligning your actions with your values ensures that you live a life of purpose and integrity, contributing to a sense of fulfilment and satisfaction.

Devotion as a Path to Knowledge:

Devotion, often understood as a deep commitment or love for a higher power or spiritual truth, can serve as a powerful path to acquiring profound knowledge. While intellectual pursuits and philosophical inquiries are crucial for understanding complex concepts, devotion adds a unique dimension to this journey. It transforms abstract knowledge into lived experience, fostering a deeper connection with the divine or universal truths. Devotion is characterised by a heartfelt commitment, reverence, and surrender to a higher power, divine principle, or spiritual truth. In various spiritual traditions, devotion is seen not just as worship but as a means to transcend the ego and attain higher understanding.

- Establish a profound relationship with the divine or universal truths.
- Allow devotion to guide personal transformation and deepen insight.
- Merge spiritual practices with intellectual pursuits for a comprehensive understanding.

Engage in regular prayer or meditation focused on seeking divine wisdom or understanding. These practices can open the mind to higher insights and foster a deeper connection with spiritual knowledge. Use guided meditations that emphasise enlightenment or divine guidance to enhance your experience. Include the study of sacred texts or spiritual literature in your routine. Devote time to reading and reflecting on these texts, approaching them with reverence and an open heart. Reflect on how the teachings relate to your personal experiences and aspirations. Adopt spiritual practices that resonate with your devotion, such as chanting, rituals, or acts of service. These practices can help internalise the principles you are studying and create a lived experience of spiritual truths.

Develop personal rituals that reinforce your commitment and connection to your spiritual path. These could include daily offerings, ceremonial activities, or symbolic acts that remind you of your devotion and the knowledge you seek. Cultivate a sense of surrender and trust in the process of seeking knowledge. By letting go of personal ego and control, you open yourself to receiving deeper insights and wisdom that transcend individual understanding. Engage with a community of like-minded individuals who share your spiritual or philosophical interests. Participating in group discussions, services, or study groups can provide new perspectives and deepen your understanding through collective wisdom.

Spend time in reflection and contemplation on the insights gained through devotional practices. Consider how these insights apply to your life and how they contribute to your overall understanding of spiritual truths. Apply the knowledge gained through devotion to your daily life. Integrate the insights into your actions, decisions, and interactions, demonstrating how devotion can translate into practical wisdom and ethical behaviour.

Begin each study or learning session to connect with divine wisdom. This could involve a short prayer or affirmation that aligns your purpose with spiritual seeking. Approach learning with mindfulness and reverence. See each new piece of knowledge as a gift from the divine or universal consciousness, and approach it with gratitude and respect. Create a balanced routine that integrates both intellectual study and devotional practices. Allocate time for reading and analysis, as well as for prayer, meditation, and other spiritual activities. Embrace the idea of continuous spiritual and intellectual growth. Recognise that devotion and knowledge are ongoing processes that evolve with time, and remain open to new insights and understandings.

Devotion can provide a more profound and experiential understanding of spiritual truths, going beyond intellectual comprehension to a lived experience. Fostering a deep connection with a higher power or universal principles can lead to greater clarity and insight into the nature of existence and one's purpose. Devotion can shift your perspective from a purely rational or analytical approach to one that encompasses emotional and spiritual dimensions, leading to a more holistic view of knowledge. The integration of devotion and knowledge promotes personal growth, helping you develop virtues such as humility, compassion, and wisdom. Living in alignment with both spiritual and intellectual pursuits can lead to a greater sense of fulfilment and purpose, enhancing overall well-being and satisfaction.

Devotion in Daily Actions:

Devotion, often associated with religious or spiritual practices, can be a transformative force in daily life. When applied to everyday actions, it fosters a sense of purpose, mindfulness, and alignment with one's core values. Devotion in daily actions isn't confined to grand gestures; it permeates every aspect of life, influencing how we approach tasks, interact with others, and align our behaviour with our deeper beliefs. Devotion in daily actions involves integrating a sense of reverence, commitment, and purpose into everyday activities. It means performing tasks with a genuine sense of care and alignment with one's values, rather than merely going through the motions. This practice infuses routine activities with greater significance, transforming them into opportunities for spiritual and personal growth.

Align your daily actions with your core values and beliefs. Infuse your daily routines with a sense of devotion by incorporating practices that align with your values. For example, if health is a priority, approach your exercise and meal preparation with dedication, viewing these actions as expressions of self-care and respect for your body. Include small acts of kindness in your daily routine. Whether it's offering a compliment, helping a colleague, or supporting a friend, these actions can be expressions of devotion and compassion. They not only positively impact others but also reinforce your commitment to living a life aligned with your values. Cultivate a sense of devotion by expressing gratitude for the opportunities and experiences of daily life. Acknowledge the significance of each moment and the lessons it offers. Regularly practising gratitude enhances your awareness of the value in everyday actions and reinforces a positive mindset.

Approach even the smallest tasks with devotion and attention. Whether it's making your bed, organising your workspace, or completing routine chores, performing these tasks with care and intentionality demonstrates respect for your environment and yourself. Consistency in small actions fosters a sense of discipline and commitment. Look for opportunities to serve others as part of your daily routine. This could involve volunteering, assisting a colleague, or contributing to community initiatives. Service-oriented actions align with the principle of devotion by focusing on the well-being of others and making a positive impact.

Establish personal rituals that embody your sense of devotion. This could include starting your day with a brief meditation, engaging in a morning affirmation practice, or dedicating time to a hobby or passion that brings you joy. Rituals create moments of connection and reinforce your commitment to living a devoted life. Ensure that your daily actions are in harmony with your long-term goals and aspirations. Regularly assess how your activities contribute to your overarching objectives and adjust your approach as needed. This alignment enhances your sense of purpose and reinforces your dedication to personal growth.

Performing daily actions with devotion brings a sense of fulfilment and satisfaction, as each task is approached with intention and purpose. Devotion fosters mindfulness, encouraging a deeper connection to each moment and enhancing overall awareness. Aligning daily actions with personal values reinforces your commitment to those values and strengthens your character. Acts of kindness and intentional interactions enhance relationships, fostering positive connections and a supportive community. A devoted approach to daily actions builds resilience by helping you stay focused on your goals and values, even in challenging situations.

Apply devotion in your professional life by approaching tasks with dedication, fostering a positive work environment, and supporting colleagues. Infuse your interactions with family and friends with intention and care, focusing on building meaningful connections and expressing appreciation. Dedicate time to personal growth activities, such as reading, learning, or pursuing hobbies, with a sense of purpose and commitment. Engage in community activities or volunteer work with a spirit of service and devotion, contributing to the well-being of others.

Sincerity in Seeking Knowledge:

Sincerity in seeking knowledge is a profound and transformative approach to learning that transcends superficial engagement. It involves a genuine commitment to understanding, integrating, and applying knowledge in meaningful ways. This sincerity is characterised by earnest curiosity, humility, and an unwavering dedication to truth and personal growth. Sincerity in seeking knowledge involves more than just acquiring facts or skills; it is about fostering a deep, authentic connection with the subject matter. This sincerity is reflected in the way one approaches learning: with openness, diligence, and a commitment to personal and intellectual integrity. It requires a mindset that values understanding and is driven by a genuine desire to grow and evolve.

Approach learning with a sense of wonder and curiosity. Ask questions not just for the sake of answers, but to deeply understand the underlying principles and implications. This curiosity fuels a more engaged and sincere approach to acquiring knowledge. Define your purpose for seeking knowledge. Whether it's for personal development, professional advancement, or intellectual enrichment, having a clear intention helps guide your learning journey and ensures that your efforts are aligned with your goals. Embrace a mindset of lifelong learning. Recognise that knowledge is not a destination but a continuous journey. Stay committed to expanding your understanding and skills, even beyond formal education or initial learning experiences.

Move beyond passive consumption of information by actively engaging with the material. This can include discussing concepts with others, applying what you've learned in practical scenarios, or teaching others. Active learning enhances comprehension and retention and demonstrates sincere engagement with the subject matter. Acknowledge the limits of your current knowledge and remain open to new perspectives. Sincerity involves recognising that there is always more to learn and being willing to adjust your views based on new information. This humility fosters a deeper and more authentic connection to learning.

Engage with a variety of sources and viewpoints to gain a more comprehensive understanding. Sincerity in seeking knowledge involves being open to different perspectives and integrating diverse insights into your learning process. Resist the temptation to take shortcuts or rely on superficial sources. Sincere learning requires a commitment to thorough research, critical thinking, and deep analysis. Avoid relying on quick fixes or easy answers and instead strive for a well-rounded and nuanced understanding. Uphold ethical standards in your pursuit of knowledge. This includes respecting intellectual property, avoiding plagiarism, and being honest about the sources and methods used in your research. Ethical integrity reinforces the sincerity of your learning process.

Sincere engagement with knowledge leads to a more profound understanding of the subject matter. This depth of insight enhances your ability to apply and integrate knowledge effectively. A sincere approach to learning fosters personal development and self-awareness. It encourages continuous growth and evolution, contributing to a more fulfilling and enriched life. Genuine curiosity and commitment to learning drive sustained motivation. This intrinsic motivation supports a consistent and dedicated approach to acquiring and applying knowledge. Active and sincere learning improves critical thinking and problem-solving abilities. By deeply engaging with concepts and seeking diverse perspectives, you develop more effective strategies for addressing challenges. Upholding ethical standards in learning reinforces integrity and respect for knowledge. This foundation supports a responsible and principled approach to acquiring and sharing information.

Develop effective study habits that reflect sincere engagement, such as setting specific learning goals, creating a structured study plan, and regularly reviewing and reflecting on the material. Apply sincerity in your professional development by seeking out growth opportunities, actively participating in training and mentorship programmes, and applying new knowledge to your work. Approach academic studies with a genuine desire to understand and excel. Engage deeply with course materials, participate actively in discussions, and seek to apply what you learn in practical ways. Pursue personal interests and hobbies with sincerity, whether it's learning a new skill, exploring a new field of knowledge, or engaging in creative projects. This approach enhances your overall well-being and satisfaction. Contribute to community learning and growth by sharing your knowledge, supporting educational initiatives, and participating in discussions and activities that promote collective understanding.

The Impact of Devotion on Mental Clarity:

Devotion inherently involves a sustained focus on a particular goal or practice. When individuals are devoted, their attention is directed towards their chosen path, reducing mental clutter and distractions. This focused attention enhances mental clarity by allowing individuals to concentrate on what truly matters to them. Devotion provides a sense of purpose, which is crucial for mental clarity. When individuals engage in activities that align with their values and beliefs, they experience greater satisfaction and motivation. This sense of purpose helps filter out irrelevant information and priorities, leading to clearer decision-making and thought processes. Devotion fosters discipline and consistency in practices or habits. Regular and disciplined engagement in devotional practices, whether it's meditation, prayer, or any dedicated activity, helps in establishing routines that promote mental clarity. Consistency reduces cognitive overload by creating structured and predictable patterns.

A committed devotional practice often leads to a sense of inner peace and contentment. When individuals find solace and fulfilment in their devotion, their minds are less disturbed by external conflicts and uncertainties. This inner peace enhances mental clarity by reducing the internal noise that can cloud thinking.

Devotion can stimulate cognitive functions by encouraging critical thinking and reflection. Engaging deeply with one's values and beliefs can lead to greater insight and understanding. This cognitive engagement sharpens mental faculties and improves clarity in both personal and professional decision-making. Incorporate regular devotional practices into your daily routine. This could be meditation, prayer, or any activity that aligns with your devotion. Consistency in practice helps train the mind to focus and reduces mental distractions.

Devotion channels attention and reduces distractions, leading to enhanced focus on tasks and goals. A sense of purpose derived from devotion provides direction and clarity in decision-making. Emotional regulation through devotion leads to reduced stress and anxiety, contributing to clearer thinking. Deep engagement with devotional practices fosters greater insight and understanding, improving cognitive clarity. Devotion provides a sense of fulfilment and contentment, leading to a clearer and more positive mindset.

Learning from Scriptures and Spiritual Texts:

Scriptures and spiritual texts serve as profound sources of wisdom, guidance, and insight, offering timeless knowledge that can deeply impact personal and spiritual growth. These texts, which vary across different cultures and religions, provide a foundation for understanding spiritual principles, ethical conduct, and the nature of existence. Learning from these sources involves more than just reading; it requires engagement, reflection, and application of the teachings to daily life.

Scriptures and spiritual texts are repositories of ancient wisdom that offer guidance on various aspects of life. They often contain teachings on ethics, morality, and spirituality, providing a framework for understanding complex concepts and making informed decisions. Engaging with these texts helps individuals gain insights into universal truths and human nature. Many spiritual texts outline principles for ethical living, such as compassion, honesty, and humility. Learning these principles helps individuals align their actions with higher values and fosters personal integrity. By applying these teachings, one can develop a strong moral compass and live in harmony with oneself and others.

Scriptures often encourage self-reflection and self-discovery. They provide tools for exploring one's inner self, understanding personal motivations, and uncovering deeper aspects of consciousness. Through practices such as meditation, contemplation, and study, individuals can gain greater self-awareness and clarity. Spiritual texts often describe practices for connecting with the divine or higher consciousness. These practices, whether through prayer, meditation, or rituals, help individuals cultivate a sense of spiritual connection and purpose. Learning from these texts can deepen one's spiritual experience and enhance personal fulfilment.

Scriptures and spiritual texts offer comfort and guidance during difficult times. They provide perspectives on dealing with adversity, finding meaning in suffering, and maintaining hope. By reflecting on these teachings, individuals can navigate challenges with greater resilience and understanding.

Dedicate regular time to study and reflect on spiritual texts. Consistent engagement allows for deeper understanding and integration of the teachings into daily life. Set aside a specific time each day or week for this practice to build a habit. Approach the texts with an understanding of their historical and cultural context. Knowing the background and purpose of the scriptures enhances comprehension and helps interpret the teachings more accurately. Utilise commentaries and scholarly resources to gain a broader perspective. Engage actively with the text by taking notes, highlighting key passages, and asking questions. Reflect on how the teachings relate to your personal experiences and challenges. This active engagement helps internalise the wisdom and apply it effectively.

Gaining knowledge from spiritual texts provides a deeper understanding of spiritual principles and practices, contributing to personal growth and enlightenment. Applying the ethical teachings from the scriptures fosters integrity, compassion, and moral behaviour, enhancing personal relationships and societal interactions. Engaging with spiritual texts promotes self-reflection and self-discovery, leading to greater self-awareness and clarity. Learning from spiritual texts deepens one's connection with the divine or higher consciousness, fostering a sense of purpose and fulfilment. Scriptures offer wisdom and comfort during difficult times, providing guidance and support to navigate life's challenges.

Devotion as a Tool for Inner Transformation:

Devotion encourages individuals to turn inward, fostering a deep self-awareness that is essential for transformation. By focusing on a higher power or spiritual ideal, individuals are prompted to examine their inner motives, desires, and values. This helps uncover and address personal weaknesses and areas for growth, leading to greater self-understanding.

Engage in the study of sacred texts or teachings that resonate with your devotional path. Learning from these sources provides valuable insights and guidance that can enhance your spiritual growth and transformation. Approach the study with an open mind and a willingness to integrate the teachings into your life. Connect with a community of like-minded individuals who share your devotional practices and goals. Engaging with others who are also on a path of transformation can offer support, encouragement, and shared wisdom. Participate in group activities, discussions, or spiritual gatherings to strengthen your devotion and personal growth.

Embrace personal sacrifices or commitments as expressions of your devotion. This may involve prioritising your spiritual practices over other activities or making changes in your life to align more closely with your spiritual ideals. Such sacrifices reinforce your dedication and contribute to inner transformation.

Devotion fosters greater self-awareness and understanding, allowing for more meaningful personal growth and transformation. The support and solace provided by devotion help build emotional resilience, enabling individuals to handle challenges with greater strength and composure. A deepened sense of devotion strengthens the connection with the divine or higher purpose, leading to a more profound spiritual experience. The inspiration from devotion encourages individuals to adopt positive behaviours and values, facilitating personal and spiritual development. Devotion provides the motivation and inner strength needed to pursue and achieve personal goals, contributing to ongoing transformation and growth.

Finding the Divine in All Knowledge:

The pursuit of knowledge has long been regarded as a sacred endeavour, a means of uncovering deeper truths about the universe and our place within it. Finding the divine in all knowledge involves recognising the inherent sacredness and interconnectedness that underpins all learning.

At its core, the concept of finding the divine in all knowledge acknowledges the interconnectedness of the universe. This perspective holds that every piece of knowledge, whether scientific, philosophical, or spiritual, is a part of a greater, unified reality. The process of discovery and learning is often seen as a sacred journey. Each new insight or understanding can be viewed as a revelation of the divine order of the universe. This sacredness imbues our intellectual pursuits with purpose and significance, aligning our search for knowledge with a higher spiritual quest. Finding the divine in all knowledge involves transcending the material aspects of learning and focusing on the underlying truths that connect us to a higher reality. This transcendence allows us to view knowledge not merely as information but as a pathway to spiritual enlightenment and connection with the divine.

Approach your studies with a sense of reverence and awareness. Recognise that each piece of information is a reflection of a greater truth and contributes to a deeper understanding of the divine. This mindfulness transforms your learning process into a spiritual practice. Explore how different fields of knowledge interrelate and reflect a unified truth. Whether studying science, philosophy, or spirituality, seek to understand how these diverse areas contribute to a cohesive understanding of the divine. This approach fosters a holistic view of knowledge. Regularly reflect on the significance of your learning journey. Contemplate how each discovery and insight brings you closer to understanding the divine order of the universe. This reflection deepens your appreciation for the sacred nature of knowledge.

Incorporate your learning into your spiritual practices. For instance, use insights from various fields to enrich your meditation, prayer, or contemplation. This integration helps bridge the gap between intellectual understanding and spiritual experience. Delve into philosophical and mystical texts that explore the relationship between knowledge and the divine. These texts often offer profound insights into how knowledge can be a path to spiritual awakening and understanding. Practice contemplative inquiry, where you meditate on and question the deeper meanings and implications of what you learn. This approach encourages you to see beyond the surface and connect with the divine essence underlying all knowledge. Sharing insights and experiences with others can enhance your understanding and provide support on your journey.

Viewing knowledge as a reflection of the divine leads to a deeper, more profound understanding of both the material and spiritual aspects of life. This holistic approach enriches your intellectual and spiritual development. Recognising the divine in all knowledge infuses your learning with a sense of purpose and meaning. This perspective aligns your intellectual pursuits with a greater spiritual quest, providing a sense of fulfilment and direction. Embracing the sacred nature of knowledge fosters a greater reverence for the learning process. This reverence enhances your engagement with the material and deepens your appreciation for the interconnectedness of all things. Finding the divine in knowledge facilitates the integration of spiritual and intellectual growth. This integration creates a balanced and harmonious approach to personal development, where both aspects complement and enrich each other. By seeing the divine in all forms of knowledge, you strengthen your connection with the higher reality that underpins the universe. This connection enhances your spiritual awareness and fosters a sense of unity with the divine.

Using Knowledge to Serve Others:

Knowledge, when applied to serve others, becomes a powerful tool for positive impact. Utilising one's expertise, insights, and understanding for the benefit of others not only amplifies the value of knowledge but also fosters a sense of purpose and fulfilment. This approach emphasises the ethical use of knowledge to address needs, solve problems, and enhance the well-being of individuals and communities.

The foundation of serving others with knowledge begins with empathy. Understanding the needs, challenges, and perspectives of others allows for the application of knowledge in a manner that is truly beneficial and respectful. Using knowledge responsibly involves adhering to ethical principles. This includes ensuring that the application of knowledge does not harm others and is used with integrity and transparency. Sharing knowledge fosters a collaborative approach where others can benefit from insights and experiences. This practice promotes mutual growth and empowers individuals and communities. Applying knowledge to solve real-world problems enhances its relevance and impact. A problem-solving mindset focuses on identifying practical solutions that address specific needs.

Apply knowledge to initiate or participate in community projects that address local challenges. Whether it's developing sustainable practices, improving healthcare, or supporting education, community projects leverage expertise to create tangible benefits.

This contribution provides valuable support to causes that align with your expertise. Provide consulting services or advisory support to individuals or organisations seeking guidance. This can include offering strategic advice, problem-solving solutions, or specialised knowledge to help them achieve their goals. Mentor or coach individuals seeking personal or professional development. Sharing your knowledge and experiences helps guide others in their growth journey, fostering their skills and confidence.

Serving others with knowledge provides a sense of purpose and fulfilment. The act of contributing to the well-being of others enriches one's own life and fosters a deeper connection with the community. Applying knowledge to address challenges and solve problems results in tangible benefits for individuals and communities. This positive impact reinforces the value and relevance of knowledge. Serving others through knowledge fosters trust and strengthens relationships. Building connections based on shared knowledge and mutual respect enhances collaboration and support.

Teaching and sharing knowledge with others often deepens one's understanding. The process of explaining concepts and addressing questions reinforces and expands one's knowledge base. By addressing local challenges and providing support, knowledge application empowers communities. This empowerment leads to improved quality of life and greater self-sufficiency. Ensure that knowledge is applied with cultural sensitivity and respect. Understanding and addressing cultural differences is crucial for effective and respectful service.

Summary:

In this chapter, we learned about the balance between knowledge and devotion, and how both can guide us on the spiritual path. The journey from knowledge to wisdom involves not just learning facts but understanding and applying them in daily life. We explored how spiritual and philosophical knowledge can be used practically, helping us live more meaningful lives. Devotion, or sincere love for the divine, is shown as a path to gaining knowledge, and transforming everyday actions into acts of devotion.

Sincerity in seeking knowledge is essential, and devotion helps clear the mind, making it easier to grasp deeper truths. By learning from scriptures and spiritual texts, we grow both intellectually and spiritually. Devotion is a tool for inner transformation, allowing us to see the divine in all forms of knowledge. Finally, we learn that true knowledge should be used to serve others, turning learning into a way to benefit the world.

Part III – ACHIEVE

Chapter 7 – Finding Purpose

Source: lewisginter.org

"Life is a pilgrimage. The wise man does not rest by the roadside inns. He marches direct to the illimitable domain of eternal bliss, his ultimate destination."

–Swami Vivekananda

Life is a journey or pilgrimage, where a wise person doesn't get stuck at temporary stops along the way. Instead, they keep moving toward their true goal, lasting happiness and peace. This means that while there are distractions and short-term pleasures, real purpose and joy come from staying focused on what truly matters and not settling for less. The ultimate aim is to find deeper meaning and contentment in life.

Understanding the Concept of Life Purpose:

Understanding the concept of life purpose is important for personal fulfilment and a meaningful existence. Life purpose refers to the central motivating aim of an individual's life, the driving force behind their actions, decisions, and aspirations. It encompasses a deeper sense of direction and significance, guiding how one navigates life's challenges and opportunities. It is directly linked with personal values, passions, and the impact one wishes to make in the world.

Life purpose can be described as the fundamental reason for one's existence, encompassing the unique contributions and experiences that give meaning to life. It is more than just setting goals or achieving success; it involves understanding and embracing what makes one's life feel meaningful and fulfilling. Identifying this purpose often requires introspection and self-awareness to align one's actions with their core values and passions.

Ask yourself questions like, "What activities make me lose track of time?" and "What values are most important to me?" Journaling can be a useful tool to document your thoughts and insights. Experiment with various activities and interests to identify what resonates with you. This might include trying new hobbies, volunteering, or pursuing educational opportunities. Pay attention to what activities bring you joy and fulfilment. Seek feedback from friends, family, and mentors. Others' perceptions of your strengths and passions can provide valuable insights into your life purpose. They may notice qualities or talents in you that you might overlook.

Make choices that align with your life purpose. Evaluate opportunities and decisions based on how well they support your overall sense of meaning and fulfilment. Prioritise activities and relationships that contribute to your purpose. Recognise that the journey to discovering and living your life purpose may involve setbacks and challenges. Practice self-compassion and resilience to navigate obstacles and stay committed to your path.

Allocate time for activities that align with your purpose. Create a balanced schedule that includes time for personal growth, passion projects, and activities that bring you joy and fulfilment. Engage in projects or initiatives that reflect your life purpose. This might include career endeavours, community service, or creative pursuits. Ensure that these projects are meaningful and contribute to your sense of purpose. Practice mindfulness to stay connected with your purpose throughout daily activities. Being present in the moment helps you align your actions with your core values and maintain a sense of purpose.

Balancing various aspects of life can sometimes lead to conflicting priorities. Address this by prioritising your purpose and making conscious decisions that align with it, even if it means making difficult choices. If you struggle with clarity, continue exploring and reflecting. It's a process that evolves over time. Allow yourself the space to grow and adapt as you gain new experiences and insights. Societal expectations and external pressures may influence your sense of purpose. Stay true to your values and desires, and avoid letting others' expectations dictate your path.

Living in alignment with your purpose leads to greater satisfaction and fulfilment, as your actions resonate with your core values and passions. A clear sense of purpose fuels motivation and determination, helping you overcome obstacles and persist in the face of challenges.

Aligning with your purpose fosters deeper connections with others who share similar values and goals, enriching your relationships and community. The journey to discovering and living your life purpose promotes personal growth, self-awareness, and a sense of accomplishment.

Aligning Personal Values with Purpose:

Personal values are the core principles and beliefs that guide your behaviour, decisions, and interactions with others. When these values are in harmony with your life purpose, they create a powerful synergy that drives personal growth, satisfaction, and a deeper sense of fulfilment. This ensures that your daily actions and long-term goals reflect what truly matters to you, leading to a more coherent and purposeful life.

The first step in aligning personal values with your purpose is to identify your core values. These are the fundamental beliefs and principles that shape your worldview and behaviour. Create a list of potential values from a comprehensive list of common values such as integrity, compassion, creativity, or adventure. Narrow down this list to the values that resonate most deeply with you. Use values assessment tools or quizzes available online to gain additional perspectives on your core values. These tools can help you prioritise and articulate what is most significant to you.

To align your values with your life purpose, you must first have a clear understanding of your purpose. Practice self-discovery exercises, use vision boards, or guided introspection. Consider what drives you and what impact you wish to have on the world. Develop a purpose statement that succinctly describes your core mission and aspirations. This statement should reflect your passions, strengths, and the difference you want to make in the world.

Once you have identified your values and purpose, evaluate how well they align. Compare your list of core values with your purpose statement. Identify areas where they intersect and where they might diverge. This comparison will reveal if there are any discrepancies between what you value and what you are pursuing. Assess whether your daily actions and decisions align with your values and purpose. Are you living in a way that reflects your core values? If not, identify specific areas where adjustments are needed.

To achieve alignment, integrate your values into your daily routine and long-term goals. Set goals that reflect both your values and your life purpose. Ensure that your goals are designed to advance your purpose while adhering to your core principles. For example, if creativity is a core value and innovation is part of your purpose, set goals that foster creative projects and innovative solutions. Make decisions based on how well they align with your values and purpose. Before making significant choices, evaluate how they align with your core principles and how they will impact your purpose. Create an action plan that includes steps for incorporating your values into your daily life. This might involve adopting new habits, pursuing opportunities that resonate with your values, or making changes to your environment.

Schedule regular check-ins to assess how well you are living in accordance with your values and purpose. Reflect on your progress, celebrate successes, and adjust your plans as needed. Be open to adapting your values and purpose as you grow and evolve. Life experiences and personal growth may lead you to reassess your values and adjust your purpose accordingly.

Living in alignment with your values and purpose brings a deeper sense of fulfilment and satisfaction. Your actions and decisions resonate with what truly matters to you. Alignment creates consistency between your values, actions, and purpose, leading to a more coherent and integrated life experience. When your values and purpose are aligned, you are more motivated and energised to pursue your goals. Your passion for your purpose drives you to overcome obstacles and stay committed. Aligning with your values fosters authentic connections with others who share similar principles. This strengthens relationships and creates a supportive network.

Identifying Passion and Its Role in Purpose:

Identifying your passion and understanding its role in your life purpose is fundamental to achieving fulfilment and satisfaction. Passion is the intense enthusiasm and dedication you feel towards specific activities or interests, while purpose is the broader mission or goal that gives your life direction and meaning. When passion aligns with purpose, it fuels your journey, making your efforts more engaging and meaningful.

The first step in integrating passion with purpose is to discover what truly excites and motivates you. Perform activities that spark joy and curiosity. Reflect on hobbies, interests, and experiences that have brought you the most satisfaction and enthusiasm. Ask yourself what you would do if there were no limits or restrictions. Review past experiences where you felt particularly engaged or energised. Identify common themes or activities that elicited strong positive emotions.

These reflections can provide clues about your passion. Create a list of activities, interests, and causes that you are passionate about.

Once you have identified your passions, it's essential to understand how they relate to your broader life purpose. Evaluate how your passions align with your life purpose. Reflect on how your passions can contribute to or enhance your sense of purpose. For example, if your passion is for environmental conservation and your purpose is to contribute to sustainable living, these alignments can drive your actions and decisions. Integrate your passions into your daily life and long-term goals. Find ways to incorporate activities and projects related to your passions into your routine. This integration ensures that your life purpose is driven by your external goals and internal enthusiasm. Recognise that passion plays a significant role in maintaining motivation and engagement. When your work or activities align with your passions, you are more likely to persist through challenges and setbacks, as your passion provides the drive to overcome obstacles.

To fully leverage your passion in the pursuit of your purpose, establish goals that are directly related to your passions. These goals should reflect your interests and align with your broader purpose. For example, if your passion is writing and your purpose is to educate, set goals related to writing educational content or books. Actively seek out opportunities that align with your passions. Look for roles, projects, or volunteer work that allows you to engage in activities you love. This proactive approach helps you stay connected with your passions and purpose.

Maintaining passion, especially in the face of challenges, requires intentional effort. Be prepared for setbacks and challenges that may test your passion. Use these experiences as opportunities for growth and learning. Stay resilient by reminding yourself of the joy and fulfilment your passions bring. Allow your passions to evolve over time. As you grow and gain new experiences, your passions may shift or deepen. Stay open to this evolution and adjust your goals and actions accordingly.

When your passions are aligned with your purpose, you experience a deeper sense of fulfilment and satisfaction. Your work and activities become more meaningful and engaging. Passion fuels motivation, making it easier to overcome obstacles and persist in your efforts. The excitement you feel for your passions drives you to take action and achieve your goals. Pursuing passions that align with your purpose promotes personal growth. It encourages you to develop new skills, explore new interests, and expand your horizons. When you align your passions with your purpose, you are more likely to make a positive impact in areas that matter to you. Your work becomes a reflection of your core values and interests, leading to more significant contributions.

The Role of Self-Discovery in Finding Purpose:

Self-discovery is a crucial step in uncovering and understanding your life purpose. It involves a deep exploration of your inner self, values, passions, strengths, and motivations. This journey of self-awareness not only illuminates what you are truly passionate about but also aligns your daily actions with your broader sense of purpose. Let's explore how self-discovery plays a pivotal role in finding purpose and offers practical techniques to facilitate this process and finding the purpose.

Self-discovery is a reflective process that involves gaining insight into your personal identity, values, and aspirations. It is through this process that you identify what drives you and what you find fulfilling.

Key aspects of self-discovery include:

- Deep thought about your experiences, beliefs, and desires. This involves asking yourself questions like, "What are my core values?" and "What activities make me feel most alive?"
- Developing an understanding of your strengths, weaknesses, and emotional responses. Self-awareness helps you recognise patterns in your behaviour and preferences, which can guide you towards your purpose.

Several techniques can aid in the self-discovery process:

- Tools such as the Myers-Briggs Type Indicator (MBTI) or the Enneagram can provide insights into your personality traits and preferences. These assessments help you understand how your inherent qualities align with potential life paths and purposes.
- Identify and prioritise your core values through exercises like values lists or guided meditations. Understanding your values helps you make choices that are consistent with what you find most important, guiding you towards a purpose that resonates deeply with you.
- Engaging in various activities and interests to explore what you are passionate about. Experiment with new hobbies, volunteer work, or career paths. Observing what you enjoy and where you excel can offer clues about your true purpose.

Once you have gained insights through self-discovery, integrating these insights into your search for purpose, make a conscious effort to align your daily actions and decisions with your core values and passions. This alignment fosters a sense of coherence and fulfilment, reinforcing your understanding of your purpose. Based on your self-discovery insights, set long-term and short-term goals that reflect your newfound understanding of your purpose. Ensure that these goals are meaningful and resonate with your personal values and passions.

Self-discovery can be a challenging and ongoing process. Self-discovery may reveal new directions that require significant life changes. Embrace these changes as opportunities for growth and view them as steps towards a more fulfilling purpose. Doubts about your insights or the feasibility of pursuing your purpose are natural. Address these doubts by seeking support from mentors, friends, or coaches who can provide encouragement and perspective.

The process of self-discovery may not always provide immediate clarity. Be patient with yourself and allow the insights to unfold over time. Trust the process and remain open to new possibilities. Self-discovery is not a one-time event but an ongoing journey. Continuously explore new interests, learn from different experiences, and remain adaptable to new insights about yourself and your purpose.

How Purpose Shapes Personal Identity:

Purpose acts as a guiding force, influencing how we perceive ourselves, make decisions, and interact with the world. Understanding the relationship between purpose and personal identity is crucial for achieving self-awareness and aligning one's life with deeper aspirations.

Personal identity is a composite of values, beliefs, experiences, and aspirations that define who we are. Purpose, as a core aspect of this identity, provides direction and meaning to our lives. It helps clarify our values and goals and influences how we view ourselves and our place in the world.

Purpose helps to crystallise your core values. These values form the foundation of your identity and guide your behaviour and decisions. Reflect on what truly matters to you and how these values align with your sense of purpose. A personal mission statement articulates your purpose and serves as a guide for your actions and decisions. It helps in reinforcing your identity by providing a clear sense of direction and commitment to your goals. Our sense of self is deeply influenced by our purpose. It shapes how we see ourselves, our capabilities, and our role in the world. When you align your actions with your purpose, it reinforces a positive self-image and a strong sense of identity.

Regular self-reflection helps you assess whether your actions and experiences align with your purpose. This introspection strengthens your self-perception and helps you maintain a coherent sense of identity. Observe how pursuing your purpose impacts your self-esteem and confidence. Personal growth achieved through purposeful actions enhances your self-view and reinforces your identity.

Purpose plays a critical role in decision-making by providing a framework for evaluating choices and actions. When your decisions align with your purpose, they reinforce your identity and ensure consistency in how you present yourself to the world. Make decisions that reflect your sense of purpose. This alignment ensures that your choices contribute to your personal identity and help in achieving your long-term goals. Assess how your decisions impact your sense of identity. Reflect on whether the outcomes align with your purpose and contribute to your overall sense of self.

Purpose drives personal growth by challenging you to reach beyond your comfort zone and pursue meaningful goals. This growth not only enhances your skills and abilities but also reinforces your identity. Establish goals that push you to develop new skills and capabilities. Achieving these goals fosters a sense of accomplishment and strengthens your identity. Seek out opportunities for learning and development that align with your purpose. Continuous growth enhances your personal identity and supports your evolving sense of self.

Relationships are an integral part of personal identity, and purpose influences how you interact with others. A clear sense of purpose can help you build meaningful connections and strengthen your social identity. Build relationships with individuals who share your values and purpose. These connections reinforce your identity and provide support for pursuing your goals. Support others in their pursuit of purpose. Helping others can enhance your sense of identity and create a sense of fulfilment.

Implement strategies to manage stress and overcome obstacles. Resilience in the face of challenges strengthens your identity and reinforces your sense of purpose. Keep your purpose in mind during difficult times. This perspective helps you stay focused on your goals and reinforces your identity. Living authentically means aligning your actions and decisions with your true self. Purpose helps you achieve authenticity by providing a clear sense of direction and ensuring that your behaviour reflects your core values. Ensure that your actions and decisions are consistent with your sense of purpose. Authentic behaviour reinforces your personal identity and enhances your self-awareness.

The pursuit of purpose often involves creating a lasting impact or legacy. This sense of legacy shapes how you view your life and contributes to your personal identity. Reflect on the impact you want to have on the world. Make decisions and take actions that align with your desired legacy.

Exploring Different Philosophies of Purpose:

The concept of purpose has been explored and interpreted through various philosophical lenses, each offering unique insights into the nature of human existence and the meaning behind our actions. By delving into different philosophies of purpose, we can gain a broader understanding of how various thinkers have conceptualised life's meaning and how these ideas can influence our search for purpose.

Existentialism, popularised by philosophers like Jean-Paul Sartre and Albert Camus, posits that life inherently lacks meaning, and it is up to individuals to create their purpose through choices and actions. Existentialists argue that the search for purpose is a personal journey, driven by the freedom to make choices and the responsibility to embrace the consequences. According to existentialism, we are free to define our purpose. This freedom requires taking responsibility for our actions and their impact on our lives and others. Camus, in his concept of the "absurd," suggests that acknowledging the inherent lack of meaning in the universe allows us to create our purpose in defiance of this absurdity.

Utilitarianism, as articulated by philosophers like Jeremy Bentham and John Stuart Mill, suggests that the purpose of life is to maximise overall happiness and minimise suffering. This philosophy emphasises the greatest good for the greatest number, guiding actions and decisions based on their impact on collective well-being.

Stoicism, a philosophy founded by Zeno of Citium and developed by thinkers like Epictetus and Marcus Aurelius, focuses on living in accordance with nature and embracing virtue as the highest good. Stoics believe that purpose is achieved by cultivating inner virtues and accepting the things we cannot control. Develop virtues such as wisdom, courage, justice, and temperance. The purpose is found in living a virtuous life and responding to external events with equanimity. Embrace what is beyond your control and focus on what you can change. This acceptance aligns with the Stoic view of purpose as living in harmony with nature.

In Hindu philosophy, the concept of dharma refers to one's duty or righteous path, which is aligned with one's role in the universe. The purpose is found in fulfilling one's dharma, which varies according to individual circumstances, caste, and stage of life. Identify and adhere to your duty or role in life. This adherence provides a sense of purpose and alignment with cosmic order. Balance material pursuits with spiritual practices, adhering to the principles of dharma to achieve fulfilment and purpose.

Buddhism teaches that the ultimate purpose of life is to attain enlightenment and liberation from the cycle of suffering and rebirth (samsara). This enlightenment is achieved through practices that cultivate wisdom, ethical conduct, and mental discipline. Engage in meditation and mindfulness to develop awareness and insight. The pursuit of enlightenment involves overcoming ignorance and delusion. Adhere to the principles of right understanding, intention, speech, action, livelihood, effort, mindfulness, and concentration to achieve spiritual growth and purpose.

Absurdism, closely related to existentialism, particularly in the works of Albert Camus, suggests that the search for meaning in a seemingly indifferent universe is inherently absurd. It advocates embracing this absurdity and creating personal meaning despite it. Recognise the inherent lack of objective meaning and find freedom in accepting this condition. Purpose is crafted through personal choices and actions in the face of absurdity. Engage fully in life's experiences, embracing the freedom to create your meaning despite the universe's indifference.

Taoism, as articulated by Laozi in the Tao Te Ching, emphasises living in harmony with the Tao, or the natural way of the universe. The purpose is found in aligning with the natural flow of life and embracing simplicity and spontaneity. Practice wu wei (non-action or effortless action) and live in harmony with the natural order. The purpose is achieved by aligning with the flow of the Tao and embracing simplicity. Seek balance in life, reflecting Taoist principles of harmony and alignment with the natural world.

Humanism, as a secular philosophy, focuses on human potential and the pursuit of personal and collective flourishing. It emphasises reason, ethics, and justice as central to finding purpose and improving the human condition. Engage in activities that enhance human dignity, freedom, and potential. Purpose is found in contributing to human flourishing and ethical progress. Work towards creating a more just and equitable society, reflecting the humanistic values of empathy, compassion, and reason.

The Impact of Purpose on Emotional Health:

Having a defined purpose helps individuals cope better with stress and adversity. When people have a sense of meaning, they are more likely to view challenges as manageable and temporary rather than overwhelming and permanent. This mindset can reduce emotional strain and improve coping mechanisms.

Purpose allows for a reframing of stressful situations as opportunities for growth. By focusing on long-term goals, individuals can perceive setbacks as part of a broader journey rather than isolated failures. A strong sense of purpose can act as a buffer against stress, providing a stable emotional foundation that helps individuals persevere through difficult times. A clear sense of purpose often correlates with higher levels of life satisfaction. When individuals are engaged in activities that align with their values and aspirations, they experience a greater sense of fulfilment and joy. Purpose-driven activities contribute to a richer and more satisfying life experience. Engaging in tasks that reflect one's purpose leads to increased happiness and contentment. Purpose helps stabilise emotional health by providing direction and focus. It offers a sense of coherence and control over one's life, reducing feelings of uncertainty and anxiety. When individuals have a sense of purpose, their life experiences are integrated into a coherent narrative. This narrative provides emotional stability and helps in making sense of life events. Purpose can mitigate anxiety by offering a sense of direction. Knowing that one's actions contribute to a larger goal can reduce feelings of fear and worry about the future.

Purpose enhances motivation and engagement, which can positively affect emotional health. When people are motivated by a sense of purpose, they are more likely to engage in activities that bring joy and satisfaction. A sense of purpose fuels motivation, leading individuals to approach tasks with enthusiasm and commitment. This proactive attitude can lead to greater emotional satisfaction and resilience. Purpose-driven engagement fosters a sense of accomplishment and satisfaction. Participating in activities that resonate with one's values enhances emotional well-being and personal fulfilment.

A sense of purpose often leads to stronger social connections, which are crucial for emotional health. People with a clear purpose are more likely to build supportive relationships and contribute positively to their communities. Purpose often involves contributing to others, leading to the formation of meaningful relationships. These connections provide emotional support and enhance feelings of belonging and acceptance. Engaging in purposeful activities that benefit others fosters empathy and compassion, enriching emotional health through positive social interactions.

Viewing life through the lens of purpose helps individuals appreciate the journey rather than just the destination. This perspective enhances emotional satisfaction and reduces feelings of emptiness. Purpose aligns daily activities with personal values, fostering a sense of integrity and fulfilment. This alignment enhances emotional well-being and contributes to a sense of peace and contentment.

Exploring the Link Between Purpose and Spiritual Growth:

Understanding the relationship between purpose and spiritual growth offers profound insights into how one's life can be enriched and aligned with deeper values and aspirations. Purpose and spiritual growth are intertwined aspects of a meaningful life, each influencing and enhancing the other.

To explore the link between purpose and spiritual growth, it's essential first to define these concepts clearly.

- Purpose is a sense of direction and meaning in life, often tied to one's passions, values, and goals. It provides a framework for making decisions and pursuing aspirations that contribute to the greater good.
- Spiritual growth involves the development of a deeper understanding of oneself and the universe. It includes expanding one's awareness, connecting with a higher power or inner self, and cultivating qualities such as compassion, humility, and inner peace.

A well-defined purpose can act as a catalyst for spiritual growth by providing a clear direction and motivation for personal development. When you pursue goals aligned with your core values and purpose, you engage in activities that foster spiritual awareness and fulfilment. When your actions align with your deeper values, you often experience a sense of inner peace and satisfaction.

This alignment can enhance your spiritual journey by connecting you with a greater sense of meaning. Pursuing a purpose that involves helping others or contributing to a cause greater than yourself can lead to profound spiritual experiences. Acts of service and compassion are often central to spiritual growth.

Connect with people who resonate with your purpose and spiritual goals. Engaging with a supportive community can provide encouragement, inspiration, and shared experiences. Join groups or organisations that focus on personal and spiritual development.

Summary:

In this chapter, we explored the concept of life purpose and its importance in shaping who we are. We learned how understanding our purpose can help align our personal values with our actions. Finding passion plays a key role in guiding us toward our purpose, and self-discovery helps us uncover what truly drives us. The chapter also discussed how having a purpose gives us a sense of identity and direction in life.

Different philosophies on purpose were explored, showing how purpose can be viewed in various ways. We also learned about the positive impact of having a clear purpose on our emotional health, giving us motivation and resilience. Finally, the chapter highlighted the connection between finding purpose and spiritual growth, showing how living with purpose can lead to a deeper, more meaningful life.

Chapter 8 – Mastering Willpower

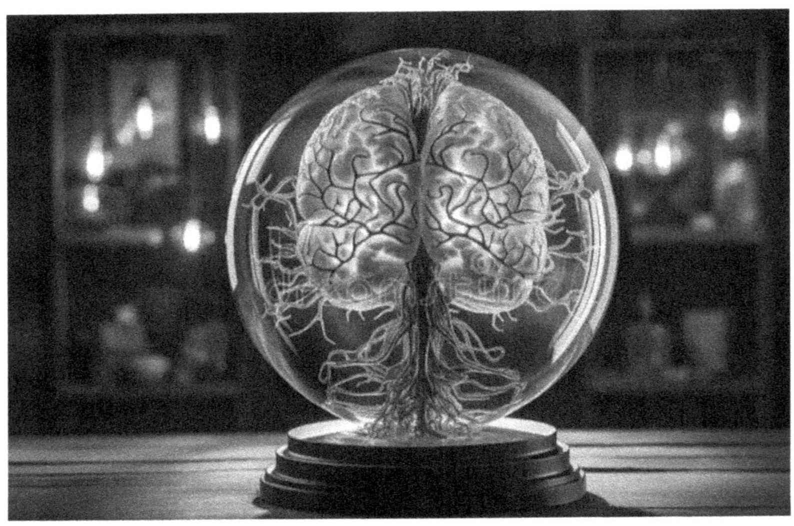

Source: dreamstime.com

> *"The only way to come up is to come up fighting."*
>
> *–Swami Vivekananda*

To overcome challenges and rise above difficulties, you need to actively fight for what you want. It highlights the importance of determination and willpower. Just like in a battle, you must stay strong, face obstacles head-on, and keep pushing forward. Mastering willpower means staying focused, not giving up when things get tough, and fighting through challenges to achieve your goals.

Understanding Willpower:

Willpower is the mental strength to carry out decisions, resist temptations, and overcome obstacles in pursuit of a goal. It is a crucial element of self-control and discipline, playing a significant role in shaping our behaviours and outcomes. Understanding willpower is the first step in mastering it and utilising it effectively in daily life. This involves exploring its nature, recognising its impact, and developing strategies to strengthen and sustain it over time.

Willpower can be seen as a finite resource, similar to a muscle that becomes fatigued with overuse. When you exert self-control, whether by resisting temptation or forcing yourself to complete a difficult task, you are tapping into this reserve of willpower. Over time, without proper replenishment, this reserve can be depleted, making it more difficult to maintain discipline and self-control. This concept, known as "ego depletion," suggests that our capacity for willpower is limited but can be managed and even strengthened through practice.

Understanding that willpower is finite helps in recognising the importance of prioritising tasks and focusing on what truly matters. By being mindful of how you expend your willpower, you can conserve energy for the most important decisions and actions.

Willpower significantly impacts every aspect of life, from making healthy lifestyle choices to achieving long-term goals. It allows you to delay gratification, stay focused, and persist in the face of challenges. When well-developed, willpower can help you break bad habits, form positive routines, and stay on track even when motivation wanes. The strength of your willpower directly influences your ability to maintain discipline and achieve success in various areas of life.

Strengthening willpower is possible through deliberate practices and lifestyle adjustments.

- Just like a muscle, willpower can be gradually strengthened by starting with small, manageable tasks. Begin by setting small goals that require discipline, such as making your bed every morning or limiting distractions for short periods. As you successfully achieve these smaller goals, your willpower will grow stronger, enabling you to take on more significant challenges.
- Creating consistent daily routines can reduce the need to make decisions that deplete your willpower. By automating parts of your day, such as meal planning or exercise schedules, you conserve willpower for more critical decisions and tasks. Routines provide structure and help prevent decision fatigue, making it easier to stay focused and disciplined.
- Willpower can be depleted, so it's essential to rest and recharge regularly. Ensure that you get adequate sleep, take breaks during the day, and engage in activities that bring you joy and relaxation. Proper rest helps restore your willpower reserves, making it easier to stay disciplined in the long run.
- Delaying gratification is a fundamental aspect of willpower. Practice delaying immediate pleasures in favour of long-term rewards. For example, instead of indulging in a snack immediately, wait for a few minutes, or choose a healthier option. Over time, this practice will strengthen your ability to resist temptations and maintain discipline.

Improving Decision-Making:

Effective decision-making is a critical skill that shapes the quality of our lives, from everyday choices to significant life-altering decisions.

The ability to make informed, thoughtful, and timely decisions can be enhanced through various techniques and practices. This section explores how to improve decision-making without overlapping with previous topics.

The decision-making process involves identifying a problem or opportunity, gathering information, evaluating options, and choosing the best course of action. It also includes the implementation of the decision and reflecting on the outcomes. Breaking down this process helps in understanding where improvements can be made.

The foundation of sound decision-making is having a clear understanding of your goals and values. When you know what you want to achieve and what is most important to you, it becomes easier to evaluate options and make decisions that align with your purpose. Regularly reflect on your values and goals to ensure they are guiding your decisions. A crucial step in decision-making is gathering relevant and accurate information. This involves researching, consulting experts, and considering different perspectives. Avoid the trap of information overload by focusing on the most pertinent data and avoiding unnecessary details. Quality over quantity should be your approach to information gathering. Developing critical thinking skills is essential for improving decision-making. This means analysing information objectively, questioning assumptions, and considering potential biases. Practice examining problems from multiple angles and evaluating the pros and cons of each option. This will help you make more rational and well-thought-out decisions.

Emotions play a significant role in decision-making, often influencing choices subconsciously. To improve your decisions, cultivate emotional awareness by recognising how your feelings may be impacting your judgement. While emotions should not be ignored, balancing them with logic and reason ensures more balanced decisions. Effective decision-making involves looking beyond immediate outcomes and considering the long-term consequences of your choices. Ask yourself how the decision will affect you, others, and your future. This perspective helps in making more sustainable and beneficial decisions.

Frameworks like SWOT analysis (Strengths, Weaknesses, Opportunities, Threats) or the Decision Matrix can help organise your thoughts and assess options systematically. These tools allow you to weigh different factors and make more informed decisions based on a structured evaluation. Mind mapping is a visual tool that helps in organising information, ideas, and options. By creating a mind map, you can see the connections between different factors, which can clarify the decision-making process and reveal potential outcomes you might not have considered otherwise.

Engage with others who have different viewpoints or expertise. Discussing your options with trusted friends, mentors, or colleagues can provide new insights and help you avoid blind spots. A diverse range of perspectives enriches the decision-making process, leading to more comprehensive and balanced outcomes. Indecision can often stem from overthinking or the fear of making the wrong choice. To combat this, set deadlines for making decisions. This creates a sense of urgency and prevents procrastination. By giving yourself a timeframe, you are more likely to make timely decisions without getting stuck in analysis paralysis.

Like any skill, decision-making improves with practice. Start by making decisions on smaller, less critical matters and gradually work your way up to more significant decisions. This practice helps build confidence and hone your decision-making abilities over time. Reflecting on past decisions provides valuable lessons for future decision-making. Analyse what worked, what didn't, and why. This reflection helps identify patterns and areas for improvement, allowing you to make better decisions in the future.

Learning from Failures: Embracing Growth and Resilience:

Failure is an inevitable part of life, but it can also be one of the most valuable learning experiences. When approached with the right mindset, failures can become stepping stones to success, offering deep insights and fostering personal growth.

The first step in learning from failure is changing your perspective on what failure means. Rather than seeing it as an endpoint or a sign of inadequacy, view failure as a natural part of the learning process. Every mistake you make is an opportunity to gain new insights, refine your approach, and grow stronger in the face of challenges.

Treat each failure as a lesson. Reflect on what went wrong and why, without judgement or self-criticism. Ask yourself, "What can I learn from this experience?" This shift in perspective turns failure into a valuable teacher rather than a source of shame. A growth mindset, as opposed to a fixed mindset, allows you to see failures as opportunities for development. When you believe that your abilities and intelligence can be developed through effort and learning, you're more likely to persevere in the face of setbacks. Embrace challenges, knowing that each one contributes to your growth. Failure often brings feelings of disappointment, frustration, or even sadness. It's important to acknowledge these emotions rather than suppress them. By facing your feelings head-on, you can process them and move forward more effectively. Allow yourself to feel, but don't let those feelings define you.

After a failure, take time to analyse the situation. What were your initial goals? What actions did you take, and where did things go wrong? This detailed review helps you understand the specific factors that contributed to the failure, enabling you to make better decisions in the future. If you experience repeated failures in a particular area, look for patterns. Are there common mistakes you're making? Identifying these patterns allows you to address underlying issues and avoid similar pitfalls in the future. Sometimes, an outside perspective can provide valuable insights that you might miss. Don't be afraid to seek feedback from others, whether it's a mentor, colleague, or friend. Constructive criticism can help you see your blind spots and offer guidance on how to improve.

Reframing is a cognitive technique that involves changing the way you interpret a situation. Instead of viewing failure as a negative outcome, reframe it as a learning opportunity or a stepping stone to success. This shift in mindset can reduce the fear of failure and increase your willingness to take risks. After analysing your failure, set new, more informed goals. Use the lessons you've learned to adjust your approach and develop a clearer, more realistic plan for moving forward. This proactive response turns failure into a catalyst for growth. Resilience is the ability to bounce back from setbacks and keep moving forward. Building resilience involves maintaining a positive attitude, staying adaptable, and focusing on long-term goals.

The more you practice resilience, the easier it becomes to navigate future failures.

Instead of only celebrating success, acknowledge the effort you put into your endeavours, even if the outcome wasn't what you expected. By valuing effort, you reinforce the importance of perseverance and persistence, which are key to overcoming failures. After each failure, create a growth plan that outlines how you'll apply the lessons you've learned. This plan should include specific actions you'll take to improve and avoid repeating the same mistakes. Review and adjust your growth plan regularly to stay on track. Cultivate gratitude for the lessons that failure brings. By focusing on the positive aspects of your setbacks, you shift your mindset from one of defeat to one of appreciation for the opportunities to grow.

Understanding Willpower Limits:

Willpower is often seen as the key to achieving goals, overcoming obstacles, and maintaining discipline. However, it's essential to understand that willpower, like any other resource, has its limits. Acknowledging and respecting these limits can help you develop a more sustainable approach to self-control, rather than relying solely on sheer force of will.

Willpower can be strengthened with practice, but it also becomes fatigued when overused. Psychologists refer to this phenomenon as "ego depletion,", which suggests that the more we exert self-control in one area, the less we have available for other tasks. For instance, if you spend the day resisting temptations or making difficult decisions, you may find it harder to stick to your exercise routine or maintain patience in the evening. Understanding that willpower is a limited resource helps to shift the focus from trying to be strong all the time to being strategic about when and how you use it. This awareness also reduces the guilt and frustration that often accompany perceived "failures" in self-discipline.

Each person's capacity for willpower varies, influenced by factors like stress, sleep, nutrition, and mental health. It's crucial to recognise your limits and respect them. Ignoring signs of mental or physical exhaustion can lead to burnout, making it even harder to exercise self-control in the future. To assess your limits, pay attention to your energy levels and emotional state throughout the day. Notice when you feel most capable of making good decisions and when you tend to give in to impulses. This self-awareness can guide you in structuring your day to make the most of your willpower.

Since willpower is limited, it's essential to prioritise where you spend it. Focus your energy on tasks that align with your long-term goals and values. For example, if improving your health is a priority, allocate your willpower to making healthy food choices and exercising, rather than trying to control every aspect of your day. Habits and routines help reduce the need for willpower by automating certain behaviours. When you establish a routine, such as exercising at the same time every day, you rely less on willpower to get started because it becomes a regular part of your schedule.

To minimise decision fatigue, reduce the number of decisions you need to make daily. For example, set out your clothes the night before, or create a to-do list with prioritised tasks. This way, you can preserve willpower for more critical decisions. Your environment plays a significant role in influencing behaviour. By designing your surroundings to support your goals, you can reduce the need for willpower. For instance, if you want to eat healthier, keep nutritious snacks readily available and remove tempting junk food from your home. If you want to focus on work, eliminate distractions from your workspace.

When you encounter setbacks, practising self-compassion can help preserve your willpower. Instead of harshly criticising yourself for a lapse in self-control, acknowledge the difficulty of the situation and remind yourself that it's okay to make mistakes. This approach reduces the emotional toll of setbacks, allowing you to bounce back more quickly. Willpower is replenished with relaxation. Ensure that you get enough sleep and take breaks throughout the day to recharge. Mindful activities, such as meditation or deep breathing, can also help restore your mental energy, making it easier to exercise self-control when needed. Building momentum with small successes can boost your willpower for larger challenges. Break down big goals into smaller, manageable tasks and celebrate your achievements along the way. These small wins reinforce your belief in your ability to succeed, making it easier to stay motivated.

One of the key aspects of understanding willpower limits is respecting those boundaries to avoid burnout. Overextending yourself by constantly pushing past your limits can lead to mental and physical exhaustion, reducing your overall effectiveness. Burnout not only depletes willpower but also impacts your emotional resilience and ability to cope with stress.

Enhancing Focus:

Focus is the mental skill that allows you to concentrate your attention on a single task, blocking out distractions and staying engaged in the present moment. In a world full of constant distractions, mastering focus is essential for productivity, creativity, and overall mental well-being. Enhancing focus involves not only minimising external distractions but also cultivating a mindset that encourages deep concentration. Below are techniques and practices to improve focus, without repeating earlier topics related to willpower or energy management.

Focus can be thought of as a skill that can be developed with practice. It requires both mental discipline and a conducive environment. By understanding how focus works, you can better equip yourself to enhance it. Focus has two main components: attention and concentration. Attention is the ability to direct your awareness to specific stimuli, while concentration is the ability to sustain that attention over time.

In contrast to multitasking, which divides your attention among several tasks, single-tasking involves focusing on one task at a time. This practice enhances your ability to concentrate deeply on the task at hand, leading to better performance and less mental fatigue. To start single-tasking, choose one task to focus on and give it your undivided attention for a set period, such as 25-30 minutes. This technique is often paired with time management strategies like the Pomodoro Technique.

One of the most effective ways to enhance focus is by creating an environment that minimises distractions. This can involve both external and internal factors. External distractions include noise, interruptions, and visual clutter, which can be reduced by working in a quiet space, turning off notifications, and organising your workspace. Internal distractions, such as wandering thoughts or stress, can be managed by practising relaxation techniques before starting work.

Like any skill, focus can be improved through practice. Mental exercises that challenge your concentration can help build this skill over time. One simple focus exercise involves choosing a small object, like a pen or a coin, and focusing on it for five minutes. Try to observe every detail of the object while keeping your mind from wandering. This exercise strengthens your ability to concentrate and can be incorporated into your daily routine. Large, complex tasks can be overwhelming and may lead to procrastination or loss of focus. Breaking tasks into smaller, more manageable steps helps maintain focus by providing a clear path forward. Each small step offers a sense of completion, which keeps you motivated and focused.

Defining clear and specific goals for each work session can help direct your focus. When you know exactly what you need to achieve, it becomes easier to maintain concentration. Break down your goals into actionable steps and focus on completing one step at a time. Taking short, regular breaks helps to refresh your mind and prevent mental fatigue, which can hinder focus. During breaks, engage in activities that help you recharge, such as stretching, walking, or deep breathing. However, be mindful not to engage in activities that can derail your focus, such as checking social media. Engaging in regular physical activity has been shown to enhance cognitive functions, including focus. Exercise increases blood flow to the brain, which can improve concentration and mental clarity.

What you eat and drink can significantly impact your focus. Foods rich in antioxidants, healthy fats, vitamins, and minerals provide your brain with the nutrients it needs for sustained concentration. Stay hydrated, as even mild dehydration can impair cognitive function and focus. Incorporate brain-boosting foods like nuts, berries, and leafy greens into your diet to support mental clarity. Adequate sleep is essential for optimal cognitive function, including focus.

Creating a personal ritual before starting work can help signal to your brain that it's time to focus. This ritual could include specific activities like lighting a candle, listening to a particular type of music, or practising deep breathing. Over time, this ritual becomes associated with deep focus, making it easier to transition into a state of concentration.

Seeking Guidance:

Seeking guidance is an essential aspect of personal development, spiritual growth, and navigating life's complexities. It involves recognising that we don't have all the answers and being open to the wisdom, experience, and perspectives of others. Whether from mentors, teachers, spiritual leaders, or trusted friends, guidance can provide clarity, support, and direction when we face challenges or are uncertain about our next steps.

One of the most valuable aspects of seeking guidance is the opportunity to see things from a different perspective. Others may offer insights that you haven't considered, helping you to understand a situation more fully. This broadened viewpoint can lead to better decision-making and a more balanced approach to life's challenges. Those who have walked a similar path before you can offer advice on what to avoid. Whether it's a professional mentor warning you of industry-specific challenges or a spiritual teacher helping you navigate inner obstacles, their guidance can save you time, energy, and unnecessary hardship.

Guidance can accelerate your personal growth by providing tailored advice and encouragement. A mentor or guide can help you identify your strengths and weaknesses, pushing you to develop. Life's journey can be difficult, and having someone to turn to for guidance provides not just intellectual insights but also emotional support. This can help you feel less alone in your struggles, giving you the confidence and strength to keep moving forward. Guidance often comes from those who have more experience in a particular area. By learning from their successes and mistakes, you can gain wisdom without having to go through the same trials yourself. This can be particularly valuable in areas like career development, relationships, or spiritual practice.

Before seeking guidance, it's important to clarify what you need help with. Whether it's a specific problem, a general feeling of being stuck, or a desire for personal growth, understanding your needs will help you find the right person to guide you. It also makes it easier for them to offer relevant advice. Not all guidance is created equal. Look for someone who has the experience, wisdom, and perspective that align with your needs. This might be a mentor in your field, a spiritual teacher, or even a trusted friend who has navigated similar challenges. Trust and respect are key components of a successful guidance relationship. When seeking guidance, it's important to approach the conversation with an open mind. Be willing to listen without judgement, even if the advice you receive challenges your current beliefs or plans. True growth often requires stepping outside of your comfort zone.

To get the most out of the guidance you receive, ask thoughtful and specific questions. Avoid vague inquiries like "What should I do?" and instead ask questions that delve into the underlying issues, such as “How can I better manage my time to achieve my goals?” or “What steps can I take to deepen my spiritual practice?”.

After receiving guidance, take time to reflect on the advice you’ve been given. Consider how it applies to your situation and whether it resonates with your values and goals. Not all advice will be immediately applicable, but thoughtful reflection can help you integrate the guidance in a meaningful way. The true value of guidance lies in applying it to your life. Take actionable steps based on the advice you receive. Whether it’s implementing a new strategy at work, adopting a new spiritual practice, or making a difficult decision, putting the guidance into action is what leads to growth and change.

If possible, maintain an ongoing relationship with your guide. Regular check-ins allow you to continue receiving support as you progress. This also allows you to update them on your progress, show appreciation for their help, and ask for further guidance as new challenges arise. Don’t feel limited to one source of guidance. You can seek advice from different mentors, books, spiritual practices, and even your intuition. This multi-faceted approach allows you to draw from a wide range of wisdom and apply it in a way that best suits your unique journey.

While seeking guidance is important, it’s also essential to maintain a sense of independence. Use the guidance you receive as a tool for growth, but don’t become overly reliant on others to make decisions for you. Ultimately, you must take responsibility for your own path. Show appreciation to those who offer you guidance. Whether through a simple thank-you, a thoughtful gesture, or by paying it forward and offering guidance to others, expressing gratitude strengthens the bond between you and your guide and acknowledges the value of their contribution to your life.

Practising Patience:

Patience is a crucial virtue that significantly impacts various aspects of our lives, including personal growth, relationships, and overall well-being. It involves the ability to endure difficult situations, wait for outcomes, and maintain a calm demeanour despite challenges. Practising patience not only helps in handling daily stressors more effectively but also fosters a more positive and resilient mindset.

Patience is more than just waiting; it's about how we handle the process of waiting. It encompasses tolerance, perseverance, and the ability to remain calm under pressure. Practising patience involves developing emotional regulation, a long-term perspective, and an understanding that not everything can be controlled or expedited.

Mindful breathing is a technique that helps centre your focus and calm your mind. When faced with a situation requiring patience, take deep, deliberate breaths. This simple practice helps reduce stress, lowers anxiety, and brings you back to the present moment. Try inhaling deeply through your nose, holding your breath for a few seconds, and then exhaling slowly through your mouth. Repeat this several times until you feel more centred and calm. One reason people struggle with patience is having unrealistic expectations about how quickly things should happen. Setting achievable goals and timelines helps manage expectations and reduces frustration. Break larger tasks into smaller, manageable steps and recognise that progress takes time. This approach not only improves patience but also enhances your overall efficiency.

Gratitude shifts your focus from what you lack to what you have. When faced with situations that test your patience, remind yourself of the positive aspects of your life. Keeping a gratitude journal where you regularly note down things you are thankful for can help you maintain a positive outlook and strengthen your ability to wait calmly. This practice can help you remain patient in challenging interactions and foster better relationships.

Certain activities are known to naturally enhance patience. Gardening, knitting, and even puzzles are examples of activities that require sustained attention and can help develop patience. Incorporate these activities into your routine to practise patience in a relaxed and enjoyable manner.

Positive self-talk involves using affirmations and encouraging statements to manage frustration and maintain a patient mindset. Replace negative thoughts, such as "This will never end," with positive affirmations like, "I am patient and resilient." This practice helps reframe your mindset and strengthens your ability to remain patient. Reflect on previous situations where you successfully practised patience. Analysing what worked well and how you felt afterwards can provide valuable insights and reinforce your ability to handle future challenges. Recognise the benefits of patience and use past experiences as motivation to continue developing this virtue.

Practice being fully present in the moment. By focusing on the here and now, you can reduce anxiety about the future and remain more patient during periods of waiting or uncertainty. Techniques such as mindfulness meditation can enhance your ability to stay grounded and patient. Incorporate patience-enhancing practices into your daily routine. Set aside time for activities that require patience, such as reading, exercising, or engaging in hobbies. Regularly practising these activities helps build and reinforce your patience over time.

Establish specific goals related to patience. For example, aim to respond calmly in challenging situations or practice waiting without frustration. Monitor your progress and celebrate small victories to stay motivated and committed to developing patience. View challenging situations as opportunities for growth rather than obstacles. Embracing difficulties with a patient mindset allows you to develop resilience and learn valuable lessons. Approach each challenge as a chance to practice and strengthen your patience.

Embracing Continuous Learning:

In a world that is constantly evolving, embracing continuous learning is essential for personal and professional growth. Continuous learning is ongoing, voluntary, and self-motivated.

Pursuit of knowledge for personal development and career advancement. Continuous learning involves consistently seeking new knowledge, skills, and experiences beyond formal education. It requires a proactive mindset and an openness to exploring various sources of information, methodologies, and disciplines. Embracing continuous learning is about cultivating curiosity and integrating new insights into your daily life and work practices.

A growth mindset is the belief that abilities and intelligence can be developed through dedication and hard work. Cultivating this mindset encourages you to view challenges as opportunities for growth rather than obstacles. To foster a growth mindset, challenge your existing beliefs, seek feedback, and embrace new learning experiences.

Take advantage of various learning resources to gain new knowledge and perspectives. This includes books, online courses, podcasts, webinars, workshops, and professional networks. Explore resources from different fields to broaden your understanding and apply new concepts to your personal and professional life.

Invest in professional development opportunities to enhance your skills and knowledge within your field. Engaging in professional development helps you stay current with industry trends and advance your career. Seek out mentors, coaches, and peers who can provide valuable insights and guidance. Apply new knowledge and skills to real-life situations to reinforce your learning. Implementing what you have learned in practical contexts helps solidify your understanding and demonstrates the value of continuous learning. For example, if you learn a new project management technique, use it in your current projects to evaluate its effectiveness. Keep abreast of developments and trends in your field or areas of interest. Subscribe to industry newsletters, follow relevant blogs and influencers, and participate in online discussions.

Summary:

In this chapter, we explored the concept of mastering willpower and its role in personal growth. We learned how willpower helps in improving decision-making by staying disciplined and focused. The use of rewards and incentives was discussed as a way to strengthen motivation. We also examined how learning from failures helps build resilience and enhances willpower. Managing energy levels was highlighted as important to maintaining strong willpower, along with understanding its limits to avoid burnout. Enhancing focus and seeking guidance from mentors were identified as key strategies for staying on track. Patience was emphasised as an essential part of mastering willpower while embracing continuous learning helps us grow and adapt. Overall, the chapter provided practical tools to improve willpower and stay committed to long-term goals.

Chapter 9 – Achieving Goals

Source: kids.britannica.com

"Take up the idea. Make that one idea your life – think of it, live on that idea. Let the brain, muscles, nerves, every part of your body, be full of that idea, and just leave every other idea alone. This is the way to success."

–Swami Vivekananda

To reach your goals, you must commit fully to one idea or objective. By making that idea the central focus of your life, you channel all your energy, thoughts, and efforts toward it. Every part of your being, your brain, body, and mind, should be aligned with that goal while ignoring distractions or other ideas. This single-minded focus and determination leads to success by keeping you constantly moving toward your goal without being sidetracked.

Creating a Vision Board:

A vision board is a powerful tool for visualising and manifesting your goals and aspirations. By creating a tangible representation of your dreams and objectives, you can harness the power of visualisation to stay motivated and focused. It is a visual representation of your goals and desires. It typically consists of a collage of images, words, and symbols that represent what you want to achieve in various areas of your life, such as career, health, relationships, and personal development. The purpose of a vision board is to serve as a constant reminder of your goals, helping to keep you inspired and aligned with your desired outcomes.

A vision board helps clarify your goals by providing a visual representation of what you want to achieve. This clarity allows you to focus your efforts and make decisions that align with your objectives. Seeing your goals and aspirations depicted visually can boost motivation and inspire you to take action. The constant visual reminder keeps your goals at the forefront of your mind. A vision board enhances the practice of visualisation by making it more concrete. Visualisation is a powerful tool for achieving goals, as it helps you imagine the successful realisation of your aspirations. A vision board also reinforces positive thinking and beliefs. By regularly viewing your goals and affirmations, you cultivate a positive mindset and strengthen your belief in your ability to achieve your objectives.

- Begin by clarifying your short-term and long-term goals. Consider various aspects of your life, such as career, health, finances, relationships, personal growth, and leisure. Write down specific, measurable, and realistic goals for each area.

- Collect materials for your vision board. You will need a board or canvas (physical or digital), magazines, printouts, markers, glue, or design software if creating a digital vision board. Choose materials that resonate with you and reflect your personal style.

- Look for images, words, and symbols that represent your goals and aspirations. Cut out or print pictures, quotes, affirmations, and other visual elements that resonate with your objectives. Choose visuals that align with your desired outcomes.

- Arrange the selected images and words on your board. Start by placing the most important elements in prominent positions. Experiment with different layouts and designs until you find a composition that feels inspiring and meaningful to you.

- Personalise your vision board by adding your drawings, doodles, or handwritten affirmations. Incorporate elements that reflect your unique personality and style. This personal touch makes the vision board more engaging and connected to your own experiences.

- Place your vision board in a visible location where you will see it regularly, such as your workspace, bedroom, or living area. The visibility of your vision board ensures that you are constantly reminded of your goals and can stay focused on achieving them.

- Make a habit of engaging with your vision board daily. Take a few moments each day to reflect on the images and affirmations, visualise yourself achieving your goals, and reinforce your commitment. This daily engagement strengthens your connection to your aspirations and helps maintain motivation.

- Periodically review and update your vision board to reflect any changes in your goals or priorities. As you achieve certain goals, replace them with new ones to keep your vision board relevant and aligned with your evolving aspirations.

- Include positive affirmations on your vision board to reinforce your beliefs and intentions. Affirmations are powerful statements that help shape your mindset and actions. Use affirmations that resonate with your goals and foster a positive outlook.

Develop actionable steps and strategies to achieve the goals depicted on your vision board. Break down each goal into smaller tasks and create a timeline for completing them. Regularly review and adjust your action plans as needed. Monitor your progress toward achieving your goals. Keep a journal or use a tracking app to record milestones, challenges, and achievements. Tracking progress helps you stay accountable and provides a sense of accomplishment. Use your vision board as a tool for maintaining optimism and resilience, especially when facing setbacks or obstacles.

Breaking Goals into Smaller Steps:

Breaking goals into manageable, actionable steps is crucial for effective progress and achievement. A structured approach can turn daunting objectives into attainable milestones, making the journey towards your goals more focused and less overwhelming. One effective method to achieve this is by integrating the principles of the Ikigai philosophy, which is a Japanese concept that combines passion, mission, vocation, and profession to find purpose and fulfilment in life.

The term "Ikigai" translates to "reason for being" and represents a holistic approach to finding purpose and satisfaction in life. It intersects four core areas:

1. What You Love (Passion): Activities and goals that bring you joy and fulfilment.
2. What You Are Good At (Profession): Skills and talents that you excel in.
3. What the World Needs (Mission): Areas where your efforts can address needs or problems in the world.
4. What You Can Be Paid For (Vocation): Opportunities that provide financial rewards and practical benefits.

By aligning your goals with these four areas, you create a balanced, purpose-driven approach to breaking down and achieving them.

1. Begin by clearly defining your primary goal. Ensure it aligns with your overall vision and purpose. For instance, if your goal is to become a successful entrepreneur, this will be the primary focus.
2. Identify aspects of the goal that excite and motivate you. For example, if you love innovation and creativity, your entrepreneurial goal should include elements that allow you to express these passions.

- What You Are Good At: Assess your skills and strengths. If you are skilled in digital marketing, incorporate this expertise into your goal by focusing on building a strong online presence for your business.

- What the World Needs: Consider how your goal can meet a need or solve a problem. If there is a gap in the market for eco-friendly products, tailor your entrepreneurial efforts to address this need.

- What You Can Be Paid For: Ensure your goal has practical and financial viability. Evaluate how you can monetise your skills and passions, such as through offering valuable services or products.

3. Break Down the Goal into Smaller Steps:

   - Set Short-Term Objectives: Start by breaking down your primary goal into short-term objectives. For instance, if your goal is to launch a startup, your short-term objectives might include market research, business planning, and securing funding.

   - Create Actionable Tasks: Further divide each short-term objective into actionable tasks. For example, under "market research," you might include tasks such as conducting surveys, analysing competitors, and identifying target audiences.

   - Establish Milestones: Set specific milestones for each objective. These milestones will serve as checkpoints to assess progress and make necessary adjustments. For instance, a milestone could be finalising your business plan within three months.

4. Align Steps with Ikigai:

   – Integrate Passions: Ensure that each step and task aligns with what you love. This alignment will keep you motivated and engaged throughout the process. For example, if you love creating content, include content creation as a key component of your marketing strategy.

   – Leverage Skills: Utilise your skills in each step of the process. If you have expertise in financial management, apply this skill to budget planning and financial forecasting.

   – Address Needs: Focus on tasks that address the needs you identified. Ensure that your actions contribute to solving a real-world problem or fulfilling a market demand.

   – Ensure Viability: Keep financial and practical considerations in mind for every step. This could involve budgeting for startup costs or evaluating the profitability of different business models.

5. Develop a Timeline and Track Progress:

   – Create a Timeline: Develop a timeline for each step and milestone. Set deadlines to keep yourself accountable and ensure steady progress towards your goal.

   – Monitor and Adjust: Regularly review your progress and make adjustments as needed. If you encounter obstacles, reassess your strategy and make necessary changes to stay aligned with your Ikigai elements.

6. Reflect and Adapt:
   - Reflect on Achievement: Periodically reflect on your progress and celebrate achievements. Recognise how each step has brought you closer to your primary goal and how it aligns with your Ikigai.
   - Adapt as Needed: Be flexible and willing to adapt your plan based on new insights or changes in circumstances. Continuous adaptation ensures that your goal remains relevant and achievable.

Tracking Intermediate Goals:

Tracking intermediate goals is a crucial aspect of achieving long-term objectives. By focusing on and monitoring these smaller milestones, you can maintain momentum, make necessary adjustments, and stay aligned with your overarching goals.

Begin by clearly defining your intermediate goals. These are the smaller, actionable targets that lead you towards your ultimate objective. Ensure each intermediate goal is Specific, Measurable, Achievable, Relevant, and Time-bound (SMART). Implement a tracking system that suits your preferences and needs. This could be a physical planner, a digital tool, or a combination of both.

- Using Spreadsheets: Use spreadsheets to create a visual representation of your goals, deadlines, and progress. You can use formulas to automatically update progress and visualise data through charts.
- Project Management Apps: Tools like Trello, Asana, or Monday.com allow you to create tasks, set deadlines, and

track progress. These platforms offer features such as reminders, progress bars, and collaboration options.

- Goal-Setting Apps: Use apps that are specifically designed for tracking goals and milestones, offering various features like progress tracking, reminders, and motivational feedback.

Establish a routine for reviewing and updating your progress. Depending on the complexity of your goals, this could be daily, weekly, or monthly. Regular check-ins help you stay focused, make timely adjustments, and celebrate achievements. For example, if you're working on a fitness goal, you might track progress weekly through workout logs and performance metrics.

Incorporate visual indicators to track your progress:

- Progress Bars: Visual bars that fill up as you complete tasks, providing a clear indication of how much work remains.
- Checklists: Lists where you can tick off completed tasks, offering a sense of accomplishment and clarity on remaining steps.
- Milestone Markers: Designate specific milestones along your journey and track their completion. This helps in recognising significant achievements and adjusting your path if needed.

Regularly assess your performance against the set intermediate goals. Evaluate how well you are meeting deadlines, achieving targets, and staying aligned with your long-term objectives:

- Performance Metrics: Track key performance indicators (KPIs) relevant to your goals. For example, if your goal is to improve sales, monitor metrics such as conversion rates and revenue growth.

- Reflection and Analysis: Reflect on what is working well and identify any challenges or obstacles. Analyse your strategies and make necessary adjustments to stay on track.

Based on your performance evaluation, be prepared to adjust your strategies and tactics. If you encounter setbacks or changes in circumstances, modify your approach to ensure continued progress. For instance, if a marketing strategy isn't delivering the expected results, consider alternative methods or tweak your approach to better align with your target audience. Accountability plays a key role in tracking and achieving goals. Share your intermediate goals with a mentor, coach, or accountability partner who can provide support, feedback, and encouragement. Regular check-ins with your accountability partner can help maintain focus and address any issues promptly.

At each milestone, take time to reflect on what you have learned and how you can apply these insights moving forward. Consider what strategies have been effective and which areas require improvement. This reflection will help refine your approach and enhance your ability to achieve subsequent goals. Keep detailed records of your progress, challenges, and adjustments. Documenting your journey provides valuable insights for future goal-setting and helps in maintaining a comprehensive view of your achievements and areas for growth.

Identifying Weaknesses:

Recognising weak areas allows for targeted improvement and helps in turning weaknesses into strengths. One of the primary steps in identifying weaknesses is through deep self-reflection. Often, others can see our weaknesses more clearly than we can. Seeking feedback from those you trust can be an effective way to uncover areas for improvement:

- Peer Review: Ask colleagues, friends, or family members for constructive criticism. Be specific in your requests; ask them to point out areas where they think you could improve.

- 360-Degree Feedback: In professional settings, consider using a 360-degree feedback system where feedback is gathered from a range of people you interact with—superiors, peers, and subordinates.

- Anonymous Surveys: If direct feedback seems challenging, consider anonymous surveys. This method allows people to provide honest input without the fear of conflict.

Failures often expose weaknesses that we may not be aware of. Analysing past failures can provide valuable insights:

- Failure Analysis: When you experience failure, break down the event step by step. Identify what went wrong and consider whether it was due to a lack of skill, knowledge, or a particular personal trait.

- Challenge Journaling: Keep a record of challenging situations you've faced and how you responded. Over time, this can reveal patterns that point to underlying weaknesses.

Various behavioural assessments and personality tests can help identify potential weaknesses by highlighting traits that may hinder your progress.

- Personality Tests: Tools like the Myers-Briggs Type Indicator (MBTI) or the Big Five personality test can provide insights into areas where your natural tendencies might create weaknesses.
- Strengths and Weaknesses Analysis: Engage in exercises like a SWOT analysis (Strengths, Weaknesses, Opportunities, Threats) to systematically evaluate your abilities.
- Emotional Intelligence (EQ) Assessments: Tests that measure EQ can help identify areas where you may struggle with empathy, self-regulation, or social skills, all of which are critical to success.

Monitoring your behaviour over time can reveal weaknesses that might not be immediately apparent.

- Behaviour Tracking Apps: Use apps that track habits and behaviours. These can provide data over time that shows where you're falling short, such as in consistency or emotional reactions.
- Automatic Journaling: Some apps allow for automatic journaling based on triggers (e.g., location-based reminders). This can help capture your responses to specific situations and uncover weaknesses.
- Time Tracking: Track how you spend your time to see where procrastination or inefficiency might be a recurring issue, indicating a potential weakness in time management.

Compare your progress against your goals to identify weaknesses that may be hindering your success:

- Progress Reviews: Regularly review your goals and assess why you may not be hitting targets. Are there specific skills or traits holding you back?
- Goal Alignment: Compare your current abilities and traits to the requirements of your long-term goals. Where do gaps exist? These gaps are likely areas of weakness that need attention.

Identify role models in your field or life and compare their strengths to your own. Where do you fall short in comparison?

- Role Model Analysis: Identify the qualities that make your role models successful. Which of these qualities do you lack? This can help pinpoint weaknesses.
- Mentorship: If possible, seek mentorship from these role models and ask them to help identify areas where you can improve.

Emotional reactions often highlight underlying weaknesses:

- Emotional Journaling: Keep track of emotional triggers and reactions. If you find yourself consistently reacting negatively in certain situations, this may point to a weakness, such as poor stress management or lack of patience.
- Meditation and Observation: Practice meditation to develop an objective awareness of your emotions. Over time, you'll notice which emotions are dominant and potentially linked to personal weaknesses.

Implementing practices that test your limits can reveal weaknesses you weren't aware of.

- Stress Tests: Put yourself in challenging situations or take on difficult tasks to see where you struggle. These stress tests can expose weaknesses in your approach, skills, or mindset.
- Simulation Exercises: In professional or academic settings, simulations or role-playing exercises can highlight areas where you may lack confidence or skill, pointing to potential weaknesses.

The willingness to recognise that you are not perfect and that there's always room for improvement is key to identifying weaknesses:

- Humility Practice: Consciously practice humility by reminding yourself that identifying weaknesses is not a sign of failure but a necessary step towards growth.
- Growth Mindset: Adopt a growth mindset that views weaknesses as opportunities for development rather than fixed traits.

Creating a Detailed Action Plan:

A well-crafted action plan serves as a roadmap for achieving your goals. It breaks down your objectives into manageable tasks and provides a clear path forward. Creating a detailed action plan requires thoughtful consideration, organisation, and commitment. This guide will help you design an effective action plan that maximises your potential for success.

The foundation of any action plan is a clear and specific goal. Start by defining exactly what you want to achieve. Be clear about what you want to accomplish. For example, instead of setting a goal to "improve fitness," specify that you want to "run a 5K race within three months." Include criteria that allow you to track your progress. How will you know when you've achieved your goal? Ensure your goal is realistic given your resources and constraints. It's important to challenge yourself, but not set yourself up for failure. Your goal should align with your broader values, priorities, and long-term objectives. Set a deadline for your goal to create urgency and focus.

Once your goal is clearly defined, break it down into smaller, actionable tasks. For example, if your goal is to write a book, milestones might include outlining the chapters, writing the first draft, and editing. Break each milestone into specific tasks. For example, under "writing the first draft," tasks could include writing 1,000 words per day, researching specific topics, or revising chapters. Determine which tasks are most important or time-sensitive and focus on those first. Prioritisation helps ensure you're working on the right things at the right time.

Map out your tasks on a calendar or timeline. This visual representation helps you see the progression of your plan and ensures you allocate enough time for each task. While it's important to push yourself, avoid setting overly ambitious deadlines that are difficult to meet. Factor in potential obstacles and setbacks when scheduling tasks. Dedicate specific blocks of time each day or week to work on your tasks. Consistent effort, even in small increments, leads to progress.

If your goal requires specific equipment, software, or materials, make sure you have everything you need before starting each task. Some tasks may require a financial investment or a significant time commitment. Plan accordingly to avoid last-minute stress. If you need help from others, whether it's guidance, feedback, or collaboration, identify those individuals and determine when and how you'll seek their support.

Set aside time each week or month to review your progress. Are you meeting your deadlines? Are there tasks that need to be adjusted? Recognise and celebrate your progress along the way. This keeps you motivated and reinforces positive momentum. If you encounter obstacles or your circumstances change, don't be afraid to revise your action plan. Flexibility is key to maintaining momentum.

Be willing to revise your tasks, deadlines, or priorities as needed. Flexibility ensures that your plan remains relevant and achievable, even as circumstances evolve. Recognise that change is a natural part of the process. By staying adaptable, you're more likely to achieve your goals despite any setbacks.

Using Technology:

In the modern age, technology plays a crucial role in helping individuals achieve their goals efficiently and effectively. By utilising various technological tools and platforms, you can streamline processes, enhance productivity, and gain valuable insights.

Technology offers a plethora of apps designed to assist with setting and tracking goals. These apps can help you break down your goals into manageable tasks, set deadlines, and monitor progress. Some tools can help you create task lists, set priorities, and track your progress. They offer features such as reminders, deadlines, and project tracking. Some apps can assist in building and maintaining positive habits related to your goals. They provide visual progress indicators and motivational reminders.

Use tools to track how you spend your time. These tools provide insights into productivity patterns and help you identify areas for improvement. Certain apps can block distracting websites and applications, allowing you to focus on your tasks.

Use software that allows you to plan, schedule, and manage projects. These tools offer features for task assignment, progress tracking, and collaboration. Some of them facilitate communication and collaboration with team members, making it easier to work together on shared goals. Data analytics tools can provide valuable insights into your progress and performance, helping you make informed decisions. They can track and analyse data related to your goals. For instance, if your goal involves increasing website traffic, these tools can provide insights into visitor behaviour and trends. Use data analytics to monitor key performance indicators (KPIs) related to your goals. This helps in understanding what strategies are working and where adjustments are needed.

Online learning platforms provide access to a wide range of courses on various subjects. Whether you need to learn a new skill or gain deeper knowledge in a particular area, these platforms can be a valuable resource. They can enhance specific skills that align with your goals. Courses often include practical exercises and certifications. Social media platforms can be powerful tools for networking, learning, and staying motivated. Advanced technologies offer immersive experiences that can aid in skill development and goal visualisation.

Managing Finances Wisely:

Effective financial management is crucial for achieving long-term stability and success. By adopting prudent financial practices and utilising various tools and strategies, you can take control of your finances and work towards your financial goals. A well-structured budget is the foundation of financial management. It helps you track your income, expenses, and savings and ensures that you live within your means.

Record all sources of income, including salary, investments, and side hustles. Use budgeting apps to automate this process. Break down your expenses into categories such as housing, utilities, groceries, transportation, and entertainment. This helps you identify areas where you can cut costs. Allocate specific amounts to each category based on your income and financial goals. Regularly review and adjust your budget as needed.

An emergency fund acts as a financial safety net for unexpected expenses, such as medical emergencies or car repairs. Aim to save three to six months' worth of living expenses. This amount provides a buffer against financial setbacks. Set up automatic transfers from your checking account to a separate savings account dedicated to emergencies. This ensures regular contributions without requiring constant attention. Use strategies like the snowball method (paying off the smallest debts first) or the avalanche method (focusing on high-interest debts) to tackle your debt systematically. Consider consolidating high-interest debt into a lower-interest loan or balance transfer credit card to reduce overall interest payments.

Investing is crucial for growing your wealth and achieving long-term financial goals. Explore various investment vehicles, such as stocks, bonds, mutual funds, and real estate. Research their risks and potential returns. Spread your investments across different asset classes to reduce risk and increase the potential for returns. Set up automatic contributions to investment accounts, such as retirement funds, to build wealth over time.

Investing wisely can help you achieve financial growth and prepare for future financial needs. Retirement planning ensures that you have sufficient funds to maintain your lifestyle after you stop working. Contribute to retirement accounts. Take advantage of employer matches and tax benefits. Estimate your retirement expenses and desired lifestyle. Use retirement calculators to determine how much you need to save each month. Regularly review your retirement plan and adjust your contributions and investment strategies as needed. Planning for retirement helps you ensure a comfortable and financially secure future.

Regularly monitoring your financial situation helps you stay on track and make informed decisions. Review your bank statements, investment accounts, and credit reports to monitor your financial health. Conduct monthly reviews of your budget, expenses, and savings goals. Make adjustments based on your financial situation and goals. Use financial planning tools to track your progress towards specific financial goals, such as saving for a down payment or paying off debt. Tracking and reviewing your finances regularly helps you stay informed and make proactive adjustments.

Consulting with financial professionals can provide valuable insights and personalised guidance. Consider working with a certified financial planner (CFP) or adviser to develop a comprehensive financial plan and investment strategy. Consult with a tax adviser to optimise your tax situation and ensure compliance with tax laws. Work with an estate planning attorney to create a will or trust and plan for the distribution of your assets. Professional advice can help you make informed financial decisions and achieve your financial goals.

Financial discipline is key to managing your finances wisely and avoiding unnecessary pitfalls. Implement strategies to control impulsive spending, such as waiting 24 hours before making non-essential purchases. Educate yourself about personal finance and stay updated on financial news and trends. Define clear, achievable financial goals and regularly review your progress towards them. Maintaining financial discipline helps you stay focused on your goals and make sound financial decisions.

Seeking Inspiration:

Inspiration acts as a catalyst for personal growth, creativity, and achieving your goals. Whether you're working on a project, pursuing a new endeavour, or simply seeking a boost in motivation, finding sources of inspiration can profoundly impact your journey. Diverse sources can provide the spark you need to ignite creativity and motivation.

Read books on topics that intrigue you or biographies of individuals you admire. Literature can offer new perspectives, ideas, and insights that inspire you. Explore various forms of art and music. Art can evoke emotions and ideas, while music can uplift and energise you. Visit art galleries, attend concerts, or listen to different genres to find what resonates with you. Spend time in natural settings. Nature's beauty can inspire creativity and provide a sense of calm and clarity. Take regular walks in parks, go hiking, or simply sit in a garden.

Exploring new experiences can open up new sources of inspiration and creativity. Visit new places, whether locally or internationally. Experiencing different cultures, landscapes, and environments can provide fresh perspectives and ideas. Take up new hobbies or learn new skills. Challenging yourself with new experiences can stimulate creativity and inspire new ideas. Engage in volunteer work or community service. Helping others and contributing to causes you care about can provide a sense of purpose and inspire you to make a difference.

Adjusting Strategies:

Adjusting strategies is a vital aspect of achieving goals and enhancing effectiveness. As circumstances change and new information becomes available, it's essential to adapt your approach to stay aligned with your objectives and maximise success. Before making adjustments, it's crucial to evaluate your current strategies to understand their effectiveness and identify areas for improvement.

Analyse the results of your current strategies to determine their effectiveness. Look at key performance indicators (KPIs), milestones, and outcomes to assess what's working and what isn't. Recognise any challenges or obstacles that have arisen. These could be internal factors like resource limitations or external factors like market changes that are impacting your strategy's success. Seek feedback from team members, stakeholders, or mentors. Their perspectives can provide valuable insights into how well the strategy is performing and where adjustments may be needed.

Stay informed about changes in your industry or market. Trends, technological advancements, and shifts in consumer behaviour can impact the relevance of your strategies. Consider any internal changes, such as shifts in team dynamics, resource availability, or organisational priorities, that may affect the effectiveness of your strategies. Monitor external factors, such as economic conditions, regulatory changes, or competitive pressures, that could influence your strategy's success.

Engage in brainstorming sessions to generate new ideas and approaches. Encourage creative thinking and consider a variety of solutions to address the issues identified. Assess the potential impact of each alternative approach. Consider factors such as feasibility, cost, and alignment with your goals before selecting a new strategy. Test alternative approaches on a smaller scale before full implementation. This allows you to evaluate their effectiveness and make necessary refinements.

Measure the results of the new strategy against predefined KPIs and objectives. Assess whether the changes have led to improved performance and outcomes. Analyse data and feedback to understand the impact of the adjustments. Look for trends, successes, and areas for further improvement. Based on the analysis, make additional adjustments if needed. Continuously refine your strategies to ensure they remain effective and aligned with your goals.

Summary:

In the final chapter, we brought together practical strategies for achieving your goals. By creating a vision board, you can visually map out your dreams and aspirations. Breaking your goals into smaller, manageable steps helps maintain progress while tracking intermediate goals keeps you motivated. Identifying weaknesses allows for personal growth and improvement, and creating a detailed action plan ensures that each step is clear. Utilising technology and managing finances wisely are essential tools to stay on track. Seeking inspiration from others and adjusting your strategies when needed allows for flexibility and perseverance. With these approaches, you can turn your vision into reality and achieve lasting success.

Conclusion

I want to take a moment to reflect on the transformative journey we've undertaken together. Each chapter was crafted with care and intention, aimed at providing you with valuable insights and practical tools to enhance various aspects of your life. I hope that the knowledge and strategies shared have resonated with you and will serve as a guiding light on your path to personal growth and fulfilment.

We began our exploration with "self-discipline," a cornerstone of personal development. The practices we discussed - establishing routines, rising early, and integrating exercise and balanced nutrition - are essential for cultivating a productive and focused life. By emphasising the importance of self-control, consistency, and setting boundaries, we laid a solid foundation for the journey ahead. Self-discipline is not just about willpower; it's about creating a framework for success and maintaining balance in both work and personal life.

Moving forward, we delved into "physical purity", understanding how our physical well-being reflects and supports our inner state. We explored the significance of cleanliness, proper nutrition, and detoxification, and how these practices contribute to a harmonious and balanced life. The emphasis on eliminating negative habits and fostering a positive environment underscored the importance of nurturing both body and mind. By maintaining a clean and supportive living space and embracing positive influences, we create a solid base for overall well-being.

The chapter on "building stamina and physical strength" took us deeper into the realm of physical health. We discussed the importance of aerobic exercises, strength training, and flexibility, highlighting how these practices contribute to a more resilient and capable body. Through endurance training and the focus on balance and agility, we learned how to enhance our physical capabilities while also addressing areas of weakness. The integration of nature walks and proper posture emphasised the holistic approach to physical health, reminding us to respect our bodies and embrace restorative practices.

Our journey then led us to "the power of the mind," where we examined the power of mental discipline and self-knowledge. Understanding the mind's intricate functions and harnessing the power of positive thinking were key themes. We explored techniques for controlling thoughts, mastering emotions, and enhancing mental clarity. The role of imagination and creative thinking was highlighted as essential for innovation and achieving our goals. By transcending the ego and aligning our thoughts with our actions, we unlock the mind's full potential for personal growth.

In the chapter on "spiritual awakening", we delved into the deeper aspects of our existence. We explored the nature of the soul, the interconnectedness of all beings, and the role of faith in our spiritual journey. Practices such as meditation, prayer, and living in the present moment were discussed as ways to cultivate a deeper connection with ourselves. Understanding concepts like "Maya" (illusion) and the role of the Guru helped us navigate the path toward spiritual freedom and self-realisation.

Balancing "knowledge and devotion" was another key area of focus. We explored how intellectual learning and heartfelt devotion can guide us on the spiritual path. By applying spiritual and philosophical knowledge in our daily lives and viewing devotion as a transformative tool, we learned to see the divine in all forms of knowledge.

Understanding "the purpose of life" was a pivotal aspect of our exploration. We discussed how aligning personal values with our actions and discovering our passions contributes to a fulfilling and meaningful life. By examining different philosophies of purpose and recognising their impact on emotional health, we learned how a clear sense of purpose can enhance our overall well-being and spiritual growth.

In the chapter on "mastering willpower", we focused on practical strategies for strengthening our resolve and staying committed to our goals. From improving decision-making to managing energy levels and embracing continuous learning, we explored various ways to enhance willpower. The use of rewards and incentives, learning from failures, and seeking guidance were discussed as essential components of building resilience and maintaining focus.

Finally, the chapter on "achieving goals" brought together the practical aspects of turning dreams into reality. We discussed creating vision boards, breaking goals into smaller steps, and tracking progress. Identifying weaknesses, creating detailed action plans, and using technology were highlighted as key strategies for success. By seeking inspiration, adjusting strategies, and managing finances wisely, you can navigate the path toward achieving your goals with confidence and clarity.

As you close this book, I hope the insights and practices shared will serve as valuable resources in your journey. I intended to provide a comprehensive guide that addresses various facets of personal development, from physical health to spiritual growth. May you continue to apply these principles, embrace continuous learning, and strive for a balanced and fulfilling life. Thank you for being a part of this exploration. May your journey be transformative and rewarding as you pursue your goals and aspirations.

References

Vivekananda, S. (1896). Raja Yoga. London: The Theosophical Publishing House.

Vivekananda, S. (1901). The Complete Works of Swami Vivekananda (Vol. 1-9). Kolkata: Advaita Ashrama.

Goleman, D. (1995). Emotional Intelligence: Why It Can Matter More Than IQ. New York: Bantam Books.

Chopra, D. (1994). The Seven Spiritual Laws of Success: A practical guide to the fullfilment of your dreams. San Rafael: Amber-Allen Publishing.

Covey, S. R. (1989). The 7 Habits of Highly Effective People: Powerful Lessons in Personal Change. New York: Free Press.

www.ingramcontent.com/pod-product-compliance
Lightning Source LLC
LaVergne TN
LVHW021147160826
845679LV00024B/2078

* 9 7 9 8 8 9 6 1 0 1 7 0 3 *